FREE, FAIR AND EFFICIENT?

Other titles from IES:

HR Shared Services and the Realignment of HR
Reilly P
IES Report 368, 2000. ISBN 1-85184-298-5

Employee Returns: Linking HR Performance Indicators to Business Strategy
Carter A, Robinson D
IES Report 365, 2000. ISBN 1-85184-295-0

The Fifties Revival
Kodz J, Kersley B, Bates P
IES Report 359, 1999. ISBN 1-85184-288-8

From People to Profits: The HR link in the service-profit chain
Barber L, Hayday S, Bevan S
IES Report 355, 1999. ISBN 1-85184-284-5

Attendance Management: a review of good practice
Bevan S, Hayday S
IES Report 353, 1998. ISBN 1-85184-282-9

Breaking the Long Hours Culture
Kodz J, Kersley B, Strebler M T, O'Regan S
IES Report 352, 1998. ISBN 1-85184-281-0

A catalogue of these and over 100 other titles is available from IES,
or on the IES Website, www.employment-studies.co.uk

the | **Institute**
for | **Employment**
Studies

Free, Fair and Efficient?

Open internal job advertising

W Hirsh
E Pollard
P Tamkin

Supported by the IES
Research
Club

Report 371

Published by:

THE INSTITUTE FOR EMPLOYMENT STUDIES
Mantell Building
Falmer
Brighton BN1 9RF
UK

Tel.   + 44 (0) 1273 686751
Fax   + 44 (0) 1273 690430

http://www.employment-studies.co.uk

British Cataloguing-in-Publication Data

A catalogue record for this publication is available from the British Library

ISBN 1-85184-301-9

Printed in Great Britain by IKON Office Solutions plc

The Institute for Employment Studies

IES is an independent, international and apolitical centre of research and consultancy in human resource issues. It works closely with employers in the manufacturing, service and public sectors, government departments, agencies, professional and employee bodies, and foundations. For over 30 years the Institute has been a focus of knowledge and practical experience in employment and training policy, the operation of labour markets and human resource planning and development. IES is a not-for-profit organisation which has a multidisciplinary staff of over 50. IES expertise is available to all organisations through research, consultancy, publications and the Internet.

IES aims to help bring about sustainable improvements in employment policy and human resource management. IES achieves this by increasing the understanding and improving the practice of key decision makers in policy bodies and employing organisations.

The IES Research Club

This report is the product of a study supported by the IES Research Club, through which a group of IES Corporate Members finance, and often participate in, applied research on employment issues. The members of the Club are:

Anglian Water	Inland Revenue
AstraZeneca	Lloyds TSB Group
BOC Group	Marks & Spencer plc
BBC	NHS Management Executive
BT plc	Orange plc
Cabinet Office	Post Office
Department of the Environment, Transport and the Regions	Rolls-Royce plc
	Scottish Equitable
Department of Trade and Industry	Scottish Executive
Glaxo Wellcome plc	Shell UK Ltd
Halifax plc	Smiths Industries plc
HM Customs & Excise	Standard Life
HM Prison Service	Unilever UK (Holdings) Ltd
Home Office	Woolwich plc

Acknowledgements

The authors would like to thank all those who participated in this research through the workshops and mini-survey. Thanks also to Gwen Leeming at IES for organising these events and to Marks and Spencer plc and HM Customs and Excise for acting as workshop hosts. Other organisations shared their experiences, especially the Cabinet Office and the Department of Trade and Industry. Many individuals gave their time in the case study organisations: Rolls-Royce plc; HM Customs and Excise; British Gas Trading; and Halifax plc. In addition to HR professionals, many line managers and employees helped with this project, and their views were vital to the research.

Contents

Executive Summary

A quiet revolution has been taking place in large employing organisations. The internal deployment of staff by management decision has been gradually replaced by an open internal job market. In such an open system, vacancies occurring within the organisation are openly advertised to existing staff who then can choose to apply for them. Someone within the organisation, most often the manager 'owning' the vacancy, then selects the person who will fill it.

This project examined the operation of such open internal job markets to find out whether they were perceived as working effectively by both managers and staff applying for jobs. Evidence was collected from about twenty major employing organisations. In four detailed case studies, line managers and employees were interviewed as well as corporate and local HR managers.

Pressures to open up the internal job market

Many factors have encouraged employing organisations to move towards a more open internal job market. They include the devolution of personnel management to line managers; the desire for more open personnel processes and to make individuals more responsible for their own careers; and issues of 'fairness' and equal opportunities. Managers hope that a more open process will widen the candidate field, and also remind people in shortage occupations that they can pursue their careers inside their organisations as well as outside.

Unions often advocate open job filling systems and the HR function has seen it (usually mistakenly) as a means of cutting their own workload.

The concerns of users

Open internal job markets have been generally welcomed by both managers and employees. Managers feel they can attract candidates they do not already know, and should therefore be able to make better appointments. Employees see an open system as potentially fairer and as giving them more of a chance to influence their own career direction.

However, open job markets are not without their problems, and this study has highlighted a number of them.

Line managers involved in filling vacancies are concerned about attracting the right the number and quality of applicants; the time taken to fill a job and the amount of paperwork involved; the quality of the selection decision; losing staff they might have wished to keep; and too much or too little job movement.

Employees are concerned about line managers who already have people in mind for advertised vacancies; selection processes which do not seem to take account of their track record; the possibility of getting stuck in a job for too long; the squeezing out of development through 'best fit' approaches to selection; and the lack of honest feedback and career advice.

HR managers are concerned about the rigour, transparency and fairness of the process; their own workload; groups of people or jobs for which the open system does not work well; and how to combine an open job market with succession planning.

Key issues

Slow and labour intensive

All in all, an open job system takes longer and generates more work than a manager simply deciding who they want to appoint. However, this study found a wide variation in time taken, from processes which could take as little as three weeks to some which routinely took three months.

Electronic communication is already improving efficiency by using intranets to post job ads and, in some organisations, moving to on-line job applications. Employees want systems which can be easily interrogated to find the kinds of vacancies they are looking for, and would appreciate systems which could alert them when particular kinds of job vacancies come up. Some organisations are moving to employees putting CVs on-line to support their job applications. This could reduce repeated form-filling. Automated shortlisting is of interest to employers, but over-mechanical systems which just search for key words in applications will have little credibility.

Rules driving out judgement

A system which is operated mainly by local managers needs some framework of rules to regulate it. Such procedures normally define what a job ad should contain, how long it should be advertised for, what goes on the application form and what other kind of information should be used in shortlisting and selection.

Most organisations select through some combination of application form, recent appraisal data, a report from the line manager and an interview. In some cases, especially in the public sector, rigid rules and scoring systems over-control the availability and assessment of information. This is especially so in systems which assess only on generic competencies and rely heavily on scorings from performance appraisal. Such over-mechanistic approaches become a kind of 'game' in which the winners are those who are good at playing the system.

Too many or too few applicants and job moves

An open market can lead to many or too few applicants. It can also exaggerate the tendency to some jobs being over-glamorised and others being seen as 'no go areas'. Managers drafting job ads need to think about whether to cast the net wide or more narrowly, depending on the likely level of interest in the job. Some staff may move too often and others may choose not to move or can get stuck. Human resource planning needs to inform views about how often staff might expect to move job, and staff need access to sensible advice on when to apply.

Fairness and diversity

Fairness is seen one of the most compelling reasons for moving to a more open job market, but staff worry about managers who are just 'going through the motions' when they already have someone in mind.

Some groups of staff are not well served by open markets, including those who have been displaced by major organisational change and who need rapid redeployment, those who are returning from career breaks or secondments, and those who seem to be frequent 'runners up' in selection processes. Part-timers can also experience difficulties. All these groups may require some special support or intervention.

Succession planning and an open market

Many large organisations have a succession planning or development review process, which identifies candidates for specific jobs either because they are the best successor or because that job move is important in the development of the individual's career experience. All the organisations participating in this research felt that such planning was important, but that they needed to be clear how it fitted with an open job market. Two approaches can be used. Either selected jobs are filled outside the open system, or identified candidates apply and compete alongside other applicants. In an interesting compromise, applicants can be told there is a preferred candidate but there is still a competition for the job.

Whether arising through succession planning or through supporting staff with other needs, the total number of 'managed' moves (*ie* those taken outside the open system) needs to be kept to a clear minority. If not, the whole system falls into disrepute.

The role of HR and quality control

The HR function normally sets up the process, but thereafter its role can vary considerably. In some organisations it is quite remote from the operation of the process but acts in a 'policing' capacity. In others, HR acts as a closer adviser to managers and employees. The latter role seems to work much better, partly because it avoids the over-reliance on excessively rigid rules to govern the quality of the selection process. HR can also then influence the process with regard to jobs which are hard to fill or people who need a move or pro-active development.

HR can also improve the quality of the process by involving people other than the line manager in selection (*eg* impartial panel members from another work area). Training for employees and managers is critical to quality, as is the regular monitoring of the outcomes of the process.

Good practice: clear communication and a sense of balance

In a field where practice is diverse, identifying 'best practice' is difficult. However, good communication is paramount in an open job system. This applies to communicating the procedure itself, communicating with and providing feedback to candidates at every stage of the process, and being open with the whole workforce about the way vacancies have been filled.

Beyond this we might add:

- A balance is needed between rules and rigour on the one hand and flexibility and efficiency on the other.

- The need to balance 'best fit' selection with an element of skill development, in the appointments being made through open competition. Job moves which are 'managed' outside the open system should be for clear purposes and limited in number.

- Line ownership should be balanced by support from the HR function in ensuring the quality of the process. This is best done by acting in an advisory, rather than policing, capacity.

- Managers need to be trained, and employees need access to career information and advice. Outcomes should be regularly monitored and the results published to staff.

It helps if the whole process is thought about as a way of taking an appointment decision, not as a set of rules to be followed.

1. Introduction: Examining Open Internal Job Markets

This report presents the findings of an IES Research Club project into the operation of open internal job markets. The phrase 'open internal job markets' hardly rolls off the tongue, so what are they, and why does their effective operation matter?

1.1 What is an open internal job market?

An open internal job market is one in which vacancies occurring within the organisation are openly advertised to existing staff who then can choose to apply for the vacant post. Someone within the organisation, most often the manager 'owning' the vacancy, then selects the person who will fill the vacancy. The appointment is made, the successful applicant moves job and their job may then be filled in turn.

To reduce the length of this report appreciably, open internal job market will be abbreviated to OIJM!

1.2 Issues arising from the shift to OIJMs

The increasing prevalence of this approach to filling vacancies was evident among major UK employers throughout the 1990s. It appeared to be related to wider changes going on in human resource management, but received much less policy or research attention than changes in reward, performance management, employee development and so on.

A change in the way jobs are allocated within an organisation affects many people and may also be difficult to reverse. Once the benefits of a more open approach have been sold to staff, they may not be willing to go back to a more closed process.

Although at first sight the shift to an open job market seems almost an administrative matter, its implementation raises some important questions for staff and their managers. Issues which came to the attention of IES included some very practical ones: problems caused by getting too many or too few applicants for particular jobs, and concerns that large amounts of time were being spent by employees in making job applications and by managers in processing them.

There were also issues about how the longer term needs of the organisation could be met by a process which filled vacancies one at a time. In particular, does this approach necessarily always select the 'best' (*ie* best in the short term) candidate for the job at the expense of someone with potential who may take a while to develop (*ie* best in the longer term)?

Employers interested in increasing diversity were also interested in whether minority groups fared better under an open job market than a managed one.

These issues were of considerable interest to the members of the IES Research Club — a consortium of major UK employers — who therefore supported a small piece of empirical research into the operation and effectiveness of open internal job markets.

The project set out to address these main research questions:

- Are open internal job markets an effective and efficient means of deploying skills in the organisation?
- Do they help or hinder the skill development of the workforce?
- What are their side effects (*eg* on the amount of job movement, career paths, diversity, morale, retention *etc*.)?
- How is the process explained to users?
- What roles are played by the HR function in the operation of an open internal job market?

1.3 Project approach

Evidence on the operation of OIJMs was collected in various ways:

- Detailed case study research was conducted in four organisations: Rolls-Royce plc; HM Customs and Excise; British Gas Trading, and Halifax plc. This involved discussions with employees who had applied for jobs and managers who had filled vacancies, as well as with HR policy makers and practitioners.

- In addition, case material was provided by a further two organisations. The DTI happened to be evaluating its own internal job advertising and vacancy filling process at the time of this study, and IES was involved in supporting this review. The Cabinet Office kindly shared with us their information and perceptions of the wider experience of OIJMs in government departments and agencies.

- Three events were run for IES member organisations. The first was an open event run just before the project was commissioned and helped to set the research agenda. The second two workshops were run during the life of the project. About twenty employing organisations were involved in these two workshops, and 17 of them filled in a mini-survey on aspects of their practice.

This project was of strong interest to specific kinds of large employer. They included government departments (which had made a radical move to OIJM systems in the 1990s); organisations with a public sector ownership or history (*eg* British Gas, BT, Post Office); large financial organisations (*eg* Halifax, Woolwich); organisations with the need to deploy specialised staff, sometimes globally (*eg* Shell, Rolls-Royce). Most of those organisations involved in the research already operated a largely open internal job market. Some major employers with a history of strong personnel management were still moving towards a more open approach (*eg* Unilever, Marks and Spencer).

The findings therefore reflect the experiences of these kinds of employing organisations and may not apply to businesses of smaller scale or those in different sectors.

1.4 The structure of this report

This report starts in Chapter 2 by presenting the case studies, to give the reader a feel for the range of practices observed, and the inter-connected issues which were raised by the staff and managers interviewed.

The rest of the report draws not only on the case study organisations, but also on the experience of the wider group of organisations attending the workshops.

In Chapter 3 we look at the drivers for moving towards an open job market and a simple model of the key activities involved. We also look at which aspects of practice were similar between organisations and those which varied.

Chapter 4 highlights and explores some of practical and policy issues raised by the managers, HR professionals and employees involved in this study.

Chapter 5 draws together the findings of this research and suggests a number of key tensions which need to be held in balance in operating an OIJM.

An Appendix gives a more detailed checklist which organisations may care to use for themselves in designing or reviewing their own policies and practices.

2. Cases in Practice

This section of the report summarises the findings of the case study research undertaken in the course of this project.

IES conducted detailed fieldwork in four of the cases: Rolls-Royce plc; HM Customs and Excise; British Gas Trading and Halifax plc. In these cases, the IES team collected background information and policy documents (including sample job descriptions, application forms, *etc.*). Interviews were then conducted with both senior and local HR managers, line managers at a variety of levels, and employees. The interviews covered the mechanics of the process, how well it was understood, how well it met the needs of those filling vacancies and individuals trying to move jobs, and its general strengths and weaknesses.

A section on the Civil Service describes some features of the Civil Service context over the past few years which are relevant to the Customs and DTI cases. It also summarises perceptions from the Cabinet Office of the practical issues experienced by government departments and agencies which have moved to more open job markets.

In the case of the DTI, IES was closely involved in an in-depth review of the OIJM process. This work involved interviews with staff, HR and managers, but also an extensive questionnaire survey of over a thousand staff and the analysis of factual data from the personnel record system on the workforce, job moves and successful/unsuccessful applicants for vacancies.

Rolls-Royce

Context

Rolls-Royce is one of the UK's best known organisations: a global engineering company specialising in gas turbine technology in commercial aerospace, defence, marine and energy sectors and with a world-wide staff of around 49,000 employees, of which around 30,000 are based in the UK.

The organisation has been through several major change processes. In 1998 the company reorganised to form a matrix organisation with several customer facing businesses such as airlines, defence, energy and marine, operating alongside a number of operations units specialising in the technology that is utilised across the markets such as turbine, compressor and fan systems. Rolls-Royce also underwent a number of acquisitions during 1999, including Vickers, in seeking to strengthen their presence in their main markets.

The integration of the matrix structure has encouraged the adoption of common processes and currently the organisation is implementing a number of IT based systems to support best practice business processes.

Underpinning these business changes is an HR vision of:

'All employees acquiring the capability required by the business whilst realising their own aspirations.'

This vision is delivered through a number of HR processes, such as performance management, and career and employee development, all seeking to find the right balance between individual and organisational need and aspiration.

One of the defining features of internal job markets within Rolls-Royce is that the advertising of vacancies operates alongside a system of regular discussion forums involving managers and their teams, at which the performance, potential and development needs of the people in their organisation are reviewed in depth, and action plans are developed. These forums are known as development cells and take place throughout the business at two levels. There are **business cells** within a single business, which review career development for all employees but primarily focus on key roles and succession to these roles. Then there are **functional cells** which generally take place across businesses, and focus on the professional development of individuals within a particular discipline, and the movement of people across businesses worldwide.

The cells meet two to four times a year, starting at the core of the business or function and spreading out. Individual objectives set via a cascade from the business plan. These are fed into the cells along with various other forms of feedback, including appraisals and personal profiles: a CV which the individual and/or the manager writes, that is intended as an honest personal appraisal.

The development cell discussions cover a number of purposes. They may identify the development needs of people and may include training, job moves and secondments. They may identify individuals who could fill current vacancies; create succession plans; identify potential, and provide a vehicle for sharing best practice in employee development. It is expected that managers will feed back the information from the development cells to the individual who integrates the information into their development plan. The appraisal system also contains individual career aspiration and an assessment of development needs.

The OIJM process

As a consequence of development cells providing a vehicle for filling jobs, not all jobs are advertised. If there are several potential candidates identified though development cells, they would all be encouraged to apply. But on the whole it was felt that the majority of jobs were advertised in the organisation.

If a line manager has a vacancy they would normally discuss the possibility of recruiting with their Head of Group and Director to check on budgets and future organisational changes that may affect the decision. If it is decided that filling the post is appropriate, these discussions may be formalised via a recruitment requisition form. If approval is given, the line and/or HR will write the job description (JD) and the advert. The adverts are both electronic and in a paper format. Jobs would normally be advertised internally first, but the pool for recruitment can be set according to factors such as the job itself and knowledge of the internal labour market. The advert can be placed just for a

Figure 2.1: Rolls-Royce open internal job filling process

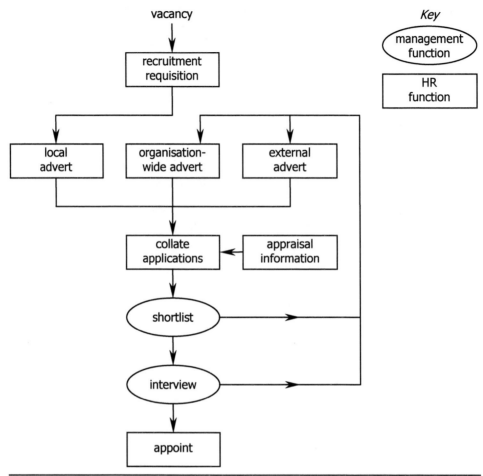

Source: IES, 2000

particular business or location, or across Rolls-Royce more widely if the line manager feels it preferable because of the expertise needed for the job.

HR collates the application with appraisal information or personal profiles and ensures the manager signs the application form.

Shortlisting is conducted by the line or HR, or both get together. HR may assist the shortlisting process by helping managers focus on the skills and competences they require for the job, using tools such as Career Architect — a proprietary system of 60 plus competences which can be prioritised to create shortlisting and selection criteria. Those shortlisted go on to interview, a decision normally based on behavioural indicators of the identified competences. Interview panels can be one or two managers plus the HR person. Everyone is trained for interviewing. Relocation costs are not normally taken into account in the selection decision.

Currently Rolls-Royce have a number of staff who are potentially surplus and is operating Resource Centres which provide a number of services to help place such people either internally or externally. Such services include advice and development on job search and placement skills, and numerous packages and other development opportunities to better understand and improve skills. Such potentially surplus staff are guaranteed an interview providing they are not clearly unsuitable.

The process was felt to be pretty well accepted. Where there is pressure, it is on the time, not on the process itself.

Once an appointment has been agreed, the current manager has the right to retain the individual for up to four weeks. If they wish to retain for longer then a mutually acceptable compromise is sought.

Apart from advertising posts, individuals can be promoted in post. The board makes the decision as to whether an individual meets the criteria for the next grade. Individuals can also take up a secondment opportunity. Secondees are the responsibility of the area they left in terms of finding them a post on return. HR keeps the secondee informed of all vacancies.

Role of HR

HR is both a catalyst and a partner in selection. It provides expert advice and brings techniques to the process, but also assists the line manager in terms of conducting selection and performing the administration. HR is a partner on sifting and interview panels, as well as ensuring all the paperwork is collated and appropriate evidence is gathered on the candidates. Some managers felt that HR's role in approving vacancies for filling was an unnecessary hurdle.

Key issues for users

The system

Generally, staff were satisfied with the system and felt that the processes were appropriate. The only negative comment was on the difficulties of securing a lateral job move. There was a desire to be able to try a move and return if it didn't work out.

Managers mentioned that they would like to be able to appoint an individual if they had identified them as their ideal candidate without going through the process. The comment was also made that some highly specialist jobs still had to be advertised internally first rather than go straight to external advert.

Managers commented that it took too long to get someone in place, but also acknowledged that when they were the losing manager they did not want to lose someone any quicker. There was general acceptance that individuals who applied for another job had to be released.

Managers commented that they could potentially let someone go and then not be allowed to fill the resultant vacancy.

Descriptions of the job

Some managers felt that job descriptions were too rigid in some cases, but changing them was difficult because they were also used for job evaluation purposes. The danger was the wrong people might be attracted to the job and the right people fail to apply.

Applications

Supervisors commented that there was only very basic detail on the application forms and therefore if the candidate was not known they had very little to base a sift decision on. It can mean they have to interview more applicants than they would like to. More senior managers commented that they would like to see a wider use of tests to help the selection decision.

The overall view was that the process was felt to be fair by staff and managers, met the needs of the organisation, and that the role of development cells was well accepted.

Key learning points

- Rolls-Royce has an established succession and development system which runs alongside open job advertising. The succession system suggests potential job moves for individuals.

- Jobs are advertised at the level that is felt to be appropriate with regard to the specifics of the job itself and the potential internal labour market. Jobs can be advertised locally, across the organisation (*ie* nationally and internationally) and finally externally.

- It is normal for line managers to release appointed individuals within four weeks and managers accept that they should release staff if successfully appointed. Variations are usually agreed on a mutual basis with all those involved.

- Assessment processes concentrate on competence based interviews and are well accepted.

British Gas Trading

Context

British Gas Trading is part of the Centrica group. Centrica is the leading supplier of energy in the UK and has a workforce almost 20,000. British Gas Trading itself has a large staff base across its Head Office in Staines and six area offices (including three call centres, two billing offices, and one national sales centre).

British Gas Trading has a history of paternalism and heavy unionisation, and management feel that some staff still look to the organisation to take care of them. They feel this is increasingly difficult since the move to privatisation and with the increased competition in the energy market, and want to manage staff expectations accordingly.

The company is starting to operate a succession planning system for more senior posts in the belief that senior posts need to be filled quickly and that organisations should plan for their potential leaders.

The OIJM process

Coverage

The organisation has different categories of staff — permanent, secondment, agency, and redeployee — which are dealt with in slightly different ways in the OIJM process. Seconded posts are filled using the internal vacancy system in the same way as permanent posts. However, staff are required to obtain their manager's permission to apply. Seconded posts may act as a stepping stone to a permanent job, as a development move, or an extended job interview.

From time to time the organisation has a number of redeployees due to periods of downsizing and reorganisation. Redeployees are given preferential treatment in the vacancy system with prior access to internally advertised vacancies. Only once the pool of redeployees has been exhausted can vacancies be opened to other staff. However, redeployees can only apply for posts at their grade. They cannot apply for promotions.

There are also a large number of agency staff in the company — estimated to make up between 30 and 40 per cent of staff at each area site. They tend to be front-line staff. Internal vacancies are generally only open to permanent staff. However, if no suitable applications are received, internal vacancies are opened up to agency staff. Agency working can therefore be a route into permanent work, acting as a probationary period. One site noted that in 1999 they converted about 100 of their 300 agency staff to permanent employees. Agency staff tend be taken on in batches (20 to 30 at a time) due to company expansion (especially in call centres), and they are assessed on job performance, sickness record and manager recommendation rather than competency based interview.

The majority of posts, both permanent and secondment, are advertised. However, the company is moving to succession planning for senior posts, which will not involve the internal vacancy system; and some lateral moves, such as 'deputising posts' where people temporarily act up, are also not advertised.

Process

Most posts are filled using the OIJM process. The process starts when a vacancy is approved — either as a secondment or permanent post. A job description is then produced and a standardised form used to draw up an advert for the post. The advert contains job information, the competencies looked for, the job description, contact information and any requirements for supporting documentation.

The advert is then placed on their network system with priority application for redeployees. Adverts are collated by HR and tend to be placed on the system once a week. Adverts are also placed on job notice boards. Adverts tend to stay on the system (board) for two weeks. Applicants request standard application forms from, and return the completed forms to, HR. The forms are rather lengthy, six pages, and are based around the identification of competencies. The form also contains a tear-off equal opportunities section, which HR detach to remove the candidate's name and sensitive information. This makes British Gas unique in ensuring line managers do not know the identity of candidates.

Figure 2.2: British Gas Trading open internal job filling process

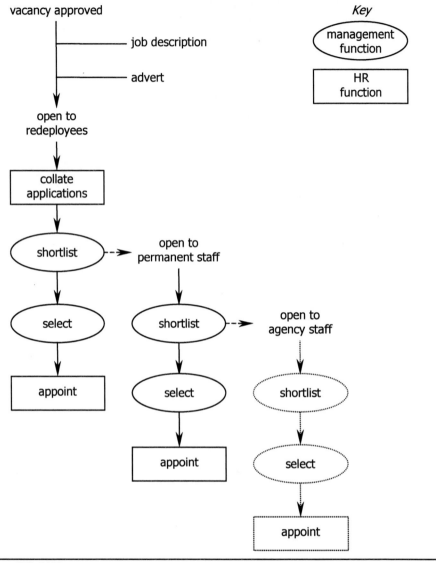

Source: IES, 2000

The anonymised application forms are then sent to the line manager of the vacancy post to shortlist by scoring forms against a standard competency framework. HR may also score a duplicate selection of forms to check for consistency. The HR function administers the selection interviews but the line manager, with a another manager, conducts the competency based panel interviews. After the interviews, a 'wash up' session is held to discuss candidates and again to check consistency of scoring. The interview panel make the selection and HR appoint the successful candidate.

The whole process can take up to two months: two to three weeks to advertise the post, a week to shortlist, a week to interview, and appoint the following week.

The company is looking to update the technology used to post vacancies, and plans to use the intranet and to allow applicants to use electronic CVs.

Role of HR

The company is organised in directorates, and each directorate has a designated Human Resource Manager — these are termed Relationship Managers. Relationship managers work closely with the line managers within their directorate and have a good understanding of the staff in their directorate. The Relationship Managers act as consultants (or coaches) to the line managers who operate the internal vacancy process and are also responsible for quality control. There are some concerns with the move to decrease the HR presence in area offices. Some staff felt that the quality of the process would deteriorate without local quality control.

Key issues for users

The process was seen as open and fair but there were concerns over its efficiency, the heavy focus on competencies, and the limited opportunities for development.

Efficiency

The process was seen as bureaucratic, as the organisation feels it needs to explain the reasons for, and consequences of, certain actions. However, the rigidity of the system does help it to be perceived as open, transparent and fair. Also, some managers felt that there were ways round the system in times of crisis, with the support of HR. The system was seen as slow. It can take up to about two months to appoint an individual, and managers and staff feel this is too long.

The system also uses old technology and is very much paper based, which allows little monitoring. Staff, HR and management wanted a more automated process to reduce the time taken to fill in application forms, to speed up the recruitment process, and to allow for better monitoring of the recruitment outcomes.

Competency focus

The job advert lists the competencies required for the post, and candidates are shortlisted, interviewed and selected on the basis of these competencies. This approach has been criticised for placing too much emphasis on competencies, leading to people 'playing the game' to win posts. Some felt the competency based interviews were too inflexible and almost ritualised. Staff would like performance data and track record also to be taken into account, and management would like technical competencies to be covered. However, the convention to interview for each post does give the system credibility.

Need for training

Staff commented that they had received no training in how to succeed in competency applications or interviews. This might be giving greater advantage to younger staff, as they are more likely to have had prior experience in this technique. However, staff felt that the standardised nature of the interviews enabled them to learn from each experience. Unlike staff, managers were given training in conducting competency based interviews and felt comfortable with this approach, which helped them to focus on what they were looking for from candidates.

Limited opportunities for development

The majority of jobs advertised are only open to those with at least six months experience at that level, and assessment is based on immediate rather than long-term potential. Managers are seen as afraid of taking risks and only making developmental appointments when no other candidate is available and as a seconded position. So development moves are rare and, when made, tend to be 'sink or swim', with individuals given little support whilst they adjust.

Learning points

- British Gas has a standardised job filling process which covers all staff/post types. However it gives priority to redeployees and also allows applications from agency staff if no suitable permanent staff are identified.

- The competency focus of the selection process can feel like an elaborate 'game' to staff, but is also seen as fair, and helps line managers focus on what they are looking for in the job. Staff wanted more account to be taken of track record.

- At British Gas, HR professionals coach line managers to operate the system and also act to ensure fair play.

- The open system restricts developmental job moves.

Halifax plc

Context

Halifax plc has a workforce of approximately 37,000 and a network of around 800 branches, 400 estate agencies and 900 agencies. In addition, the Halifax Group includes Halifax Direct, Clerical Medical, Birmingham Midshires and new Internet ventures.

The open internal recruitment policy and process was introduced in 1992 and it is currently under review. The process was originally introduced for managerial posts and has now been extended to cover all vacancies, including secondments. The open internal job market is now an integral part of the company's culture. The system has encouraged greater job movement within the organisation by increasing opportunities for development and progression. Job movement is still moderate compared to other case study organisations, predominately within and into the centre of the organisation rather than to the branch network, as a consequence of the high number of specialist and senior roles located there.

The company has recently reviewed its approach to succession planning, which runs alongside the open internal recruitment process. Succession planning within the Halifax aims to identify suitable candidates at managerial and supervisory levels, thus ensuring a sufficient number and quality of candidates to progress within the organisation. The company also operates a 'blueprinting' system (with union backing) during times of significant organisational change to ensure the most expedient and efficient redeployment of staff into new structures, taking into account their skills, capabilities and preferences.

The OIJM process

Coverage

The vast majority of vacancies are advertised internally. Some posts are also advertised externally, where specialist skills are required.

Process

The process has become slicker and quicker since its introduction. It is characterised by a standard advertising and application process combined with a flexible selection approach, significant use of IT, and the flexible involvement of HR.

Line managers are responsible for notifying personnel of a vacancy (see Figure 2.3). A standard job description is attached to the vacancy and all personnel (HR) staff are notified of the post. This enables them to provide 24 hours advanced notice of suitable vacancies to any displaced staff members. The vacancy is then displayed on the company's intranet system for a period of seven days. Interested staff access an application form via the intranet and email the completed form to the appropriate contact. The HR staff then collate the applications for shortlisting.

Although personnel assist with recruitment and selection, ultimately the responsibility for appointment lies with line management. Shortlisting is based on key skills, documented in the application form which is competency based. The selection process is flexible and uses competency based interviews. In addition, the selection process can involve psychometric tests, written assignments, role plays or presentations *etc.*, where these are relevant for the particular vacancy. Once a selection decision is made, personnel notify the successful candidate. Unsuccessful candidates are provided with individual feedback.

Each personnel team can deal with as many as 150 vacancies at any one time. Each vacancy generates an average of ten applications (more popular posts attract at least 30 applications). The length of the selection process is dependent on the particular vacancy, and in some circumstances can be as little as two and a half weeks.

The company is currently investigating the use of new technology in the internal vacancy filling process to allow greater search facilities, and to reduce users' time and effort by automatically generating information required by the process.

Role of HR

The company currently has five divisions, each with its own Business Personnel Team (BPT), providing specialist HR support to managers in implementing the company's personnel policies, such as the open internal recruitment process.

Figure 2.3: Halifax open internal job filling process

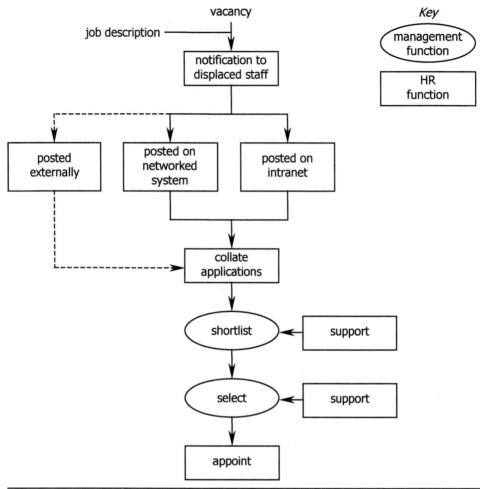

Source: IES, 2000

Business Personnel Teams ensure the smooth running of the internal recruitment process. Their role is not one of policing the system but of advising and supporting those who are using the system. The extent of personnel involvement depends on the needs and experience of the manager.

Key issues for users

The process is fast, flexible, and friendly and by and large appreciated by both empoyees and managers. Some practical issues were raised by the managers and staff interviewed. A continuous improvement programme is in operation to address these and other concerns.

Quality of applicants

Some managers interviewed were concerned that applicants do not always have the skills required for the job. They saw two reasons for this. Firstly, the centrally generated job descriptions are very general. Secondly, in spite of a broad banded grade structure introduced in 1998, some staff still relate to the old hierarchical grade structure and will apply for jobs which they perceive to be more highly graded.

Some of the staff interviewed felt there was a stigma attached to applying for jobs which do not involve promotion, and may therefore apply for jobs for which they are not well suited.

Information about jobs

Job descriptions are in a standard format and often written for job evaluation purposes rather than recruitment. Both managers and staff can find them too general and would like more information about which skills are essential and which are desirable for the particular post.

Applicants are able to obtain further information on vacancies by contacting the manager named on the advert. Managers would like to see more staff taking this initiative.

Preferred candidates

The company has conducted focus groups to address issues from staff who feel that jobs advertised on the system may have a preferred candidate for the post. Despite managers' views regarding 'on spec' applications, staff said that they did not want to spend time and energy applying for a post which they stand very little chance of getting.

Some staff prefer not to involve their managers in the application process and some fear that managers could block moves.

Flexibility

The system is not prescriptive and so allows for BPTs and managers to work closely together and to apply the most appropriate selection techniques — both for the post and for the manager.

Fast

The process from initial advertisement to the appointment of a suitable candidate is fast. As a consequence some staff would prefer a longer advertising period. However, staff are able to view recently expired vacancies and late applications may be accepted with a substantive reason.

Easy to use

The intranet system allows staff to search for jobs, access information, and e-mail applications. The process is user-friendly and utilises the company's existing systems. The process is set to become even easier to use with information automatically generated.

Learning points

- The OIJM process is flexible, especially in terms of the shortlisting and selection processes adopted. While the majority of jobs are advertised, other systems also operate in parallel, especially at times of major restructuring.

- The provision of specific and accurate job information is important to ensure good quality applications. General job descriptions produced for job evaluation purposes give the process a quick start, but may not help staff narrow down their search to those vacancies for which they are best suited.

- Even though most managers welcome a wide field of suitable applicants, staff would like to know when there is a preferred candidate. The provision of more aggregate information on the operation of the system may reassure staff that most vacancies are truly open.

- The HR function plays an advisory role which can be tailored to suit the particular needs of line managers and the requirements of the vacancy.

The Civil Service Experience

Context and the open job market process

In the past, job filling systems in the Civil Service were largely managed by the personnel function through 'grade managers', who were responsible for the deployment of specific groups of staff within a department, usually grouped by grade level. The promotion process was highly regulated, usually using promotion boards to approve the promotion of pools of staff. As job vacancies arose in a grade, staff would be appointed from the pool who had already passed the promotion board. Grading structures and pay systems were fairly uniform across the Civil Service. All staff were deemed to be generalists ('administrative') with the exception of specific groups of specialists (economists, statisticians, lawyers, scientists *etc.*). Administrative staff were accustomed to taking a very wide range of jobs, and often having several appointments at one level before progressing to the next grade.

Much has changed over the last ten years or so. Personnel management has been largely devolved to departments and agencies, with more central co-ordination for the most senior grades. Pay and grading systems have become much more diverse. The degree of discretion which line managers can use in designing, grading and filling jobs varies very much from one department to another, as does the size and role of the personnel function. Grade managers have sometimes disappeared, and sometimes remain, but usually with a modified role.

The need for more specialism in various areas of work has increased and staff have been encouraged to develop one or more areas of expertise. This trend, together with the creation of agencies and the movement of many jobs outside London, means careers are becoming more specialised. In many departments, promotion opportunities are limited.

It is against this kind of background that many departments and agencies have moved to an open job market over the last five years. The process itself varies, especially in terms of how tightly it is regulated by the personnel function. Competencies are often the basis of selection criteria. Selection panels consisting of the appointing manager plus one or two other people (sometimes including an HR manager) are widespread. Some key groups such as fast stream entrants still have managed moves, and certain specialist groups are also still more centrally managed.

Current pressures include policy initiatives to increase interchange between departments and agencies. There is also renewed attention to spotting and developing 'talent' and ensuring that more senior civil servants will have had experience of working in other sectors. Secondments are the main vehicle for achieving this.

The under-representation of women and ethnic minorities at senior levels continues to be a concern, as does the employment position of disabled people. This gives further emphasis to the need which always exists in public institutions to show that staffing practices are fair and open to scrutiny. Fairness is the dominant concern of Civil Service unions which pay close attention to job filling processes.

Perceived pros and cons of open job advertising

Against this background, how well are open job markets operating? The Cabinet Office has a role in monitoring personnel management across the Civil Service. The views summarised here are those of staff in the Cabinet Office who have received feedback on open internal job filling processes from those working on the ground in departments and agencies.

An open system for job advertising has been welcomed by both staff (and their unions) and by line managers.

Staff see the benefits as a greater choice of posts, the opportunity to apply for a wider range of jobs and general sense of fairness.

Specific problems identified by staff include:

- accuracy and quality of job descriptions. Staff feel that job specifications were sometimes drawn up with favoured candidates in mind.
- the time consuming process
- inconsistency and quality of interviewing and feedback
- lack of training for applicants and interviewers

- arrangements for returners
- average performers in competition with high flyers, and some resentment of staff who do not have to compete (*eg* fast stream entrants)
- lack of arrangements for staff who continually fail to secure jobs in competition with others
- tendency of line manages to select fully trained people rather than offer opportunities to develop
- securing moves for part-timers.

Managers are also generally positive about the open advertising system and see benefits in terms of a better choice of candidates, getting the best person for the job, and in some cases securing release. Managers also like being more involved in the process.

The downsides from a management perspective are:

- time and resources taken
- difficulty in meeting the career development needs of staff
- demotivation of staff who failed to secure a move, particularly competent performers who were regular runners-up
- the problem of staff who do not want to move.

Key learning points

- Although its history and some of its practices are different from the private sector, the Civil Service has found similar benefits and challenges in the operation of open job markets.
- The right balance between open and managed moves is a key issue, especially with the strong pressure to use more managed moves for the proactive development of talent and managing returners from secondment.
- The best mix of evidence to use in selection is also an important issue, especially in balancing track record against competency scores derived from appraisal or the application form.
- In spite of the importance of fairness and equal opportunity in the Civil Service, there is a relative lack of rigorous monitoring.
- A credible open system requires clear and open communication (including feedback to candidates) and proper training for all users (*ie* both applicants and selectors).

HM Customs and Excise

Context

HM Customs and Excise has two main businesses — UK Revenue and Anti Smuggling. Customs has a workforce of approximately 23,000 spread over a number of operational sites supported by personnel at regional level.

The organisation has run an open internal vacancy filling policy for a number of years, but the detail of operation has been through a number of changes. Trade unions are consulted on the application of the process.

One of the defining features of the Customs system compared to others we have looked at is that there are quite large numbers of job moves and certainly large numbers of individuals who are hoping for promotion or a lateral move. This places pressure on the system.

The OIJM process

As in many organisations, vacant jobs can be advertised at a number of different levels which progressively open the pool of potential applicants both in terms of current grade and location. Whilst nearly all permanent jobs are advertised, there are large numbers of project opportunities which tend not to be advertised but which can provide very important experience to individuals in readiness for potential promotion.

The process is managed at a regional level. It starts when a line manager puts in a request to fill a vacancy which is first authorised by a senior line manager and then goes to the local Human Resource Management Group (HRMG) which meets approximately fortnightly. This group has a role in determining whether posts should be filled based partly on budget considerations but also knowledge of possible surpluses of displaced staff elsewhere in the business. HRMG's role is to check over- or under-staffing at each level, and will refuse if the regional unit cannot afford to fill a post. If they do not feel that it is appropriate to fill it permanently, HR can sometimes offer to fill on temporary appointment, or they might know if there are

Figure 2.4: HM Customs and Excise open internal job filling process

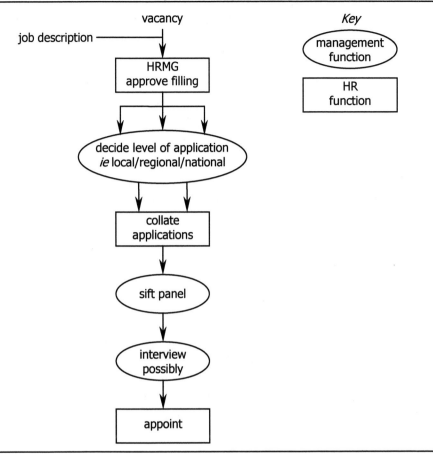

Source: IES, 2000

staffing changes in the pipeline, one of the local offices that we visited felt that refusal to fill happens around six times a year.

If filling is approved, the job goes forward and is placed in a national bulletin (one week's delay) and advertised for a minimum of three weeks.

The appointments team take the line manager's job spec, and the advert is emailed to the national bulletin. Jobs are advertised at three possible levels. Those open to only lateral moves can be advertised at level one, which can be limited to a locality, *ie* a collection. Level two is open for level moves or for promotion, and open to staff within reasonable daily travelling distance.

Level three is across band boundaries and therefore subject to national advert. The advert is, in essence, the job spec. The applications are returned to HR and associated with the individual's appraisal documents, although the number of years, worth of performance appraisal forms varies from location to location. For example, some associate two years' worth (appraisal is annual but includes a half year review).

The application form and associated performance papers are sent on to a sift panel comprising two or three trained staff, which the HR unit convene from a number of trained individuals. This may take some time to assemble due to diary constraints. Sites visited confirmed that they always have three on the panel, although there is a recommendation from HR at the centre to move to a two person sift panel when an interview will follow. Despite guidance from the centre, line managers are in some locations rarely involved and, in one, actively discouraged from taking part; similarly for interview panels.

Level transfers are decided purely by a paper sift, promotions also have an interview, but marks from the paper sift are carried forward to the interview. The interviews last about thirty minutes. Applicants are marked very good, good, suitable, unsuitable or poor against all the job criteria by each sift panellist/interviewer separately. The panellists/interviewers add all their marks together, along with any sift marks, to arrive at a final score per applicant. Within an interview panel there is a brief discussion once each panel member has awarded marks against the job criteria. If there is more than a three point difference then the panel moderates. At a certain overall mark, individuals are judged 'suitable' even if not successful. Feedback is reserved for those that are below this mark and therefore judged to be 'not suitable'. Candidates in the process felt that feedback tended to be fairly light on detail and focused on insufficient evidence of competency. Four weeks are allowed for an individual to take up the post.

The exporting manager can refuse an application if the applicant had not served the fixed time in post which was set for the job, and managers can veto the appointment on discipline or absence records.

There is a strong belief by HR and managers that practice reflects policy. HR believe that it is fair and equitable and operates rigorously. Panels do mark differently, but go to great lengths to make sure practice reflects the spirit of the guidance. Offices are encouraged to run bulk exercises where vacancies predicted for the next year are advertised. This does not seem to happen as often as might be possible because of small differences in job descriptions, or failure to plan ahead.

Role of HR

The system is unusual in the role it places on the personnel function and their ability to veto appointments. Some managers found this unnecessary, as it rarely happened, but more senior people and personnel felt that there did need to be some restraints. In essence, HR orchestrates the process, assembling panels, providing administrative support, and ensuring everything runs smoothly.

Key issues for users

Transparency

The system is perceived to be quite complex and despite the fact that it is universally applied across the organisation, staff did not understand exactly how it worked. There was some confusion over the balance between the performance at the sift panel and the performance at interview. There was a strong view expressed by applicants that the system was overly subjective and based on restricted evidence. Despite the rigor of the system, one of the most frequent complaints was that there were differences in outcome from different sift panels with similar candidates and jobs. There was a clear expectation of objectivity and therefore consistency of result.

Use of competencies

Applicants resented the fact that they were limited to evidence of competency displayed in their performance appraisal which was in turn restricted to a maximum of six competencies from a much larger list. The application form allows very restricted space for applicants' comments and therefore there was a view that it was not possible to bring in other experience gained outside of the current job. However, the organisation was attempting to manage the amount of time and effort involved in the process.

Managers were concerned at the emphasis on generic competencies, when they would have liked the ability to include technical and specialist skills in the job specification.

Use of performance appraisal

Performance assessments are a key part of the system and therefore the way in which the line manager portrays the individual is of crucial importance. This places pressure on the performance appraisal process to meet this need.

Efficiency

The process is seen as slow by all users. Staff would like to get more feedback on the progress of applications, managers would like to speed up appointments, and HR experience delays, in trying to assemble sift and interview panels. Inevitably there are delays, as there are so many steps in the process (*ie* seeking permission to fill, advertising for a fixed period and longer if potential candidates are on leave or sick, arranging the sift and possibly interview, and allowing time to take up appointment).

Feedback

Individuals wanted more feedback and feedback of more detail. Line managers felt that there were too many unsuitable candidates applying for jobs and a lack of willingness to tell people that they were not ready for a post and not support their application.

Key learning points

- There is a strong tendency for local units to take the most rigorous (and hence the most bureaucratic) option when offered flexibility.

- Line managers are less involved in the process than would normally be the case in other organisations. In some regional units they are not involved at all, in others they can be but often choose not to be.

Department of Trade and Industry

The Department of Trade and Industry (DTI) has recently carried out a review of its open internal job advertising and vacancy filling system. IES was involved in the review process and so had the opportunity to learn at first hand some of the challenges of evaluation. This case looks at how to approach evaluation as well as the findings of the DTI review.

Context and the open job market process

The DTI employs both generalist staff and specialists and has associated agencies. The open system covered by this note and by the review was introduced in 1996 and applies to the generalist staff (the large majority) who work for DTI HQ (the department excluding its agencies) — about 3,700 people as at May 1999.

The process has been modified during its first years of operation. It was also affected by a major change in grading structure implemented in 1997.

The current process is operated mainly by the line. The line manager is responsible for drafting the job advertisement, operating the selection process (within the set procedures) and providing feedback. The HR function checks and posts the job ads and circulates the paper versions. Local management units within each directorate have responsibility for the re-entry of those returning from career breaks or secondments. However, such staff still have to apply for posts through the open system. A small central HR team manages the development of specified grades of relatively senior staff although these grades still often apply for job moves through the open system.

Line managers do not have to advertise jobs which are being redeployed within a local cost centre (*ie* small unit) and at the same level. A simpler process is used for lateral moves than for jobs advertised as open for promotion. In the latter case, selection is through a panel and the line manager is responsible for finding suitable panel members. Managers and panel members should have received formal training, but this has not always the case in practice.

Conducting an evaluation

By 1999 there was a growing feeling in HR that it was time to look at how well the open system was working. Staff appeared to feel that the system was not always operated fairly (particularly with regard to women and ethnic minorities) and there were suspicions that some directorates would not appoint staff from other areas.

The evaluation was based on information collected from a variety of sources:

- focus groups and interviews with samples of managers, HR managers and employees. Unions and groups with special needs or interests (*eg* disabled staff, ethnic minorities, part-timers, returners from career breaks, secondees) were specially invited to take part in these discussions.

- a confidential questionnaire survey covering replies from nearly 1,300 staff based on a sample designed to give good representation of minority groups. The survey collected the experiences and attitudes of staff both in their capacity as applicants and, where relevant, as appointing managers. Staff completing the survey also volunteered over 600 additional comments.

- an open invitation to all staff to send in their experiences and views by e-mail or post.

- personnel records going back over several years, to examine the pattern of job moves by type of post (*eg* level, directorate, function) and type of person (*eg* age, gender, race).

- a computerised database kept of successful and unsuccessful applicants, to look at the application and success rates for different groups of staff and different kinds of posts.

The key learning points were that the 'hard' (*ie* factual data) was time-consuming to analyse (mainly because it had not been done before) but essential to producing an accurate picture of practice. The survey showed higher rates of satisfaction, especially among managers, than focus groups alone would have indicated. A survey also allowed more careful comparisons of attitudes between groups of staff and levels/functions/units.

It was important to be open from the start about the evaluation process, to welcome all input, to publish the results and to be seen to act on them.

Findings of the review

The evaluation process showed that a number of widely held negative perceptions were not supported by factual information:

- Probably about 70 per cent of posts were advertised, although staff perceived that many jobs were not openly advertised.

- The outcomes were very fair with regard to gender and race, both in terms of numbers of applications and success in competing for jobs. Indeed, at most levels women and ethnic minorities did better than white, male employees.

- The general levels and types of job movement seemed satisfactory. Half the staff had moved job in the last two years. Over 40 per cent of moves were lateral moves and about one-third of moves were between directorates (although one or two areas did appear to have a 'fortress' mentality).

- Only a very small group of staff had applied for a large number of vacancies or were blocked by their managers. Posts attracted an average of three to four applicants, and employees made on average three applications per job move.

Other key findings were:

- The long time to fill jobs — a median of 12 weeks but with some jobs taking very much longer. This was in part due to a long period of up to six weeks before hand-over.

- Part-timers did make fewer job moves, mainly because they applied for fewer posts. Older staff also moved less readily. Returners found the open system difficult as a means of re-entry.

- Managers liked some aspects of the process but wanted it to be faster, with less paperwork and with more support and advice from the personnel function. They had concerns about the quality and number of applicants being too low for some posts. Some directorates were much less popular with staff than others.

- Employees wanted clearer and more complete job information, to ensure that as many jobs as possible were advertised, and the personnel function to ensure more consistency and equality of opportunity. They wanted better access to career advice.

The results of the review have been made available to staff and discussed in depth at Board level. Action areas include a strengthening of the role of independent panel members;

shortening the time taken; improved training and guidance documentation for users; sustained monitoring; and improved career support to individuals, especially those who have trouble in securing satisfactory job moves. These changes are likely to require a slightly stronger HR influence at local level.

Key learning points

- Staff and management perceptions of an open job market can be very wide of the mark. The systematic collection and analysis of information on job moves, applicants and successful candidates is central to meaningful evaluation. This information has to be collected on an on-going basis and with thought as to how it will be analysed.

- Focus groups alone can give a biased view of staff attitudes and tend to elicit negative comments. Surveys give a more complete and balanced picture of perceptions.

- The use of independent panel members in the selection process can be an alternative to a more hands-on role for HR. It is important that they are properly trained and not 'friends' of the appointing manager.

3. An Overview of Practice

3.1 The open internal job market and what it replaces

An open job market replaces, at least in large measure, the internal deployment of staff through management decision alone. A managed job market is less transparent to staff and gives staff more restricted opportunities to influence their own deployment.

However, we must be cautious about assuming that employees had no influence in a managed market. They often made some input via the appraisal process, and there were also often individuals (usually in the personnel function) whose job it was to manage internal moves. For example, so called grade managers had this role in the Civil Service. Employees kept on the good side of their grade manager and took care to discuss job options with them when they felt it was time for a move. Some grade managers still exist in the Civil Service, especially for the more senior grades, although their role is now more concerned with managing developmental moves and secondments, than with managing every internal move.

Informal networking was as important under the managed systems of the past as it is under the more open processes of today. Employees were more likely to get a desirable move if they were known to the manager and supported by those to whom the manager looked for advice.

Under an open system, such informal systems still run side by side with the formal procedures. Finding out about a vacancy and finding sponsors is still important, and those employees skilled at managing their own careers know how to use informal networking alongside the formal OIJM processes. In the public sector in particular, there is an ambivalent attitude to this use of networking. While individuals are being encouraged to network more, formal processes still go to great lengths to give a level playing field and to exclude informal influences on the selection decision.

So the move from a managed system is a shift of emphasis. The open system places more of an onus on all employees to manage their own careers. It also involves a loss of control on the part of the organisation concerning who applies for what and when. However, managers can still seek to influence individuals to apply, just as individuals are seeking to persuade the appointing manager to appoint them.

As people tend to evaluate HR practices by comparison with what went before, views of an OIJM are partly coloured by how staff saw the previous system. In many cases, the previous system of managed moves was seen as 'putting bums on seats', and not necessarily as a subtle and careful process for balancing the needs of the organisation and the individual.

3.2 The drivers for moving to a more open system

This study has identified a number of reasons why organisations had moved to an OIJM or were considering such a move:

- the devolution of responsibility for resourcing to local unit level and away from the corporate or divisional centre. Most external recruitment had also moved this way. More central control is kept over very senior posts and high potential employees, but central deployment teams have been disbanded, so a new process is needed for filling vacancies from within.

- an accompanying shift away from the personnel function executing people management and towards line managers taking responsibility for managing their own staff. Decisions about how to fill jobs are among those going to line managers. So it seems natural for a line manager to advertise internally in order to fill their own vacancies.

- the shift away from central personnel and towards local line managers was sometimes driven by the desire to cut headcount in the personnel function. An OIJM was seen as a way of reducing the workload of the personnel function. This assumption did not always turn out to be correct.

- open internal job advertising is in tune with a desire to make individuals more responsible for their own careers. Giving employees the opportunity to choose which job they apply for is a concrete manifestation of self-managed careers.

- OIJMs are also in step with a move to more transparent HR processes. This is a wider reflection of changing attitudes to trust and authority. In many areas, employees expect more open communication and some influence on decisions affecting themselves. An open job market is one obvious way of 'empowering' individuals. Even without an open job market, employees increasingly turn down job moves suggested by their organisation, if the job or its location do not appeal.

- issues of 'fairness' and equal opportunities are seen as being better served by an open process where every employee theoretically has the same chance to put themselves forward and succeed in the selection process. 'Managed' moves, it is argued, are much more open to nepotism and therefore also to discrimination.

- in some cases, unions had been pressing for OIJM systems, although local representatives sometimes wanted movement to be open within a location or function but not across such boundaries.

- OIJMs can also be seen as a way of widening the candidate field, especially for jobs which are hard to fill. More curiously, some organisations hoped to use an open job market to increase or decrease the amount of job movement. It is not clear how they hoped this would happen. A managed job market gives the organisation much more control over the amount and types of movement taking place.

- in the case of employees who have specialist skills which are in short supply, the OIJM is seen partly as a retention measure. Such people see external job ads every day in their journals and magazines and, increasingly, on the Internet. The OIJM is a way of reminding such people that they can pursue their careers inside their organisations as well as outside.

Although the organisations involved in this research mentioned all of the drivers above, none had been all that rigorous in examining the pros and cons of moving to an open system. As with so many HR practices, there was a strong element of 'everyone else is doing it' about the shift. Although some policy goals were hoped for in the change (eg more lateral movement) it was not clear that these carried through to the detailed development of the way the OIJM system would be implemented.

As we will see later, design choices about the OIJM system, for example in the kinds of information considered in appointments and the selection criteria used, have a profound influence on which skills are valued in the workplace and what kinds of moves take place. Organisations would do better to think about some of the outcomes they are seeking, in terms of skill mix and career paths, when designing their procedures.

3.3 A series of activities

As soon as you start to talk to an organisation about its OIJM process, you realise how long it takes to describe. The main reason for this is that an OIJM process consists of a number of activities which take place in sequence. There are choices in how each step is conducted and therefore an almost endless variety of combinations of practice. Hopefully, the case studies presented in Chapter 2 have already given the reader an idea of the range of practices encountered.

We also discovered considerable variations in practice from one division or site to another within the large organisations we visited. The central personnel function was often relatively unaware of the real variation in practice on the ground.

So in presenting an overview of practice we need to simplify the picture we observed. We will do this by modelling the OIJM process as number of broad steps and then examining similarities and differences in practice within each of these blocks.

Figure 3.1 is a diagrammatic representation of the common key activities involved in an OIJM.

The first series of steps, which we call **advertisement** covers the crucial decisions about whether a vacancy should be advertised internally, externally or both, or filled in some other way. In this stage, the parameters of the job are also set and the internal advertisement is 'posted' for staff to see. This often involves decisions about which parts of the organisation will see the advertisement and which groups of staff will be eligible to apply. The decisions taken in this first stage are fundamental to the quality of the process.

The second series of steps, which we call **application** takes place between the advert being posted, and shortlisting.

Figure 3.1: The open internal job market process

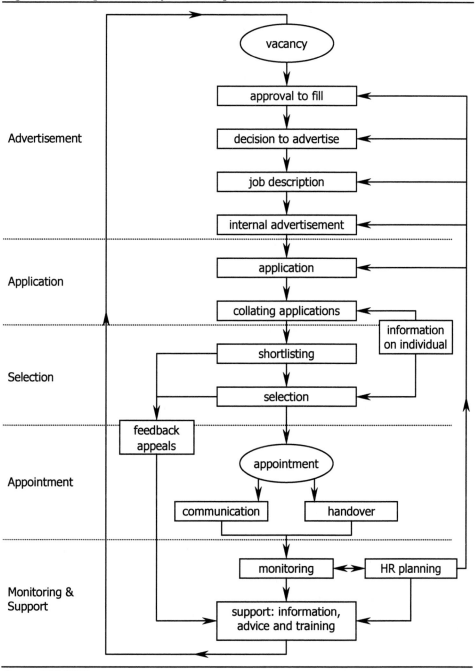

Source: IES, 2000

Most obviously, the individual applies for the job, normally on an application form. This is their key chance to put forward their case, and the design of the form can help or hinder them. Also at this stage, their boss may have to approve their application — a very sensitive issue — and may also be asked to comment on their suitability for the job. Other information can be pulled in, for example recent performance reviews.

The **selection** stage may cover a number of steps. Most often there is both a shortlisting process and interviews before the selection decision is made. There may also be other information collected from records, other people who know the candidates, tests, assessment centres, succession plans *etc.* Sometimes the same people are involved in both shortlisting and selection decisions, sometimes not. An often-neglected activity at the end of the selection stage is feedback to all those who applied on how they performed. Some organisations also have formal appeals procedures for questioning an appointment decision.

The **appointment** is then implemented. Issues arise here about informing the wider workforce of the decision, and about how an individual leaves one post to take up another. Hand-over proved one of the most contentious aspects of an OIJM process and is discussed further in section 4.5.

On the bottom of Figure 3.1 are a set of activities covering **monitoring and support**. Data need to be collected at the earlier stages to enable monitoring with respect to the quality and consistency of the process, and the fairness of outcomes. Support is also required in terms of clear information on how the process operates. Managers can benefit from guidance at several stages of the process, and some individual employees need more guidance than others on what jobs to apply for. Training in the operation of the process and in more general career management skills underpins the effective operation of the process.

The box labelled 'HR planning' merits a word of explanation. Without some link between the OIJM and workforce planning, the organisation is giving up its ability to correct imbalances in the internal labour market. Information about skill shortages and surpluses ought to feed back to the drafting of job ads and the setting of selection criteria. Succession planning may also generate information which can influence the advertising and job filling process, and is discussed further in Chapter 4. The results of monitoring should also link back to adjustments in the process.

3.4 Similarities and differences in practice

In this section, we look at the main stages and other selected aspects of the process, and highlight where practices were similar between organisations and where they differed. This information is drawn from the case studies, workshops and a mini-survey. Where proportions of companies are given they refer to those taking part in the mini-survey.

3.4.1 Advertisement

Organisations differed in whether managers needed permission before they could fill a vacancy internally.

Most organisations claimed they sometimes advertised groups of similar jobs together.

There were considerable variations in the proportion of vacancies advertised in the populations covered by the process, from about 50 per cent up to 95 per cent. About half the organisations surveyed did not advertise their most senior jobs, although the level of jobs advertised tended to rise once the process was embedded and therefore these exempted populations were often very small.

Where succession planning or organisational career reviews were conducted, these could lead to jobs being filled outside the OIJM process. In other organisations, the post would still be advertised but the ad would make clear there was a preferred candidate. This same approach could be used where a local candidate was already known to the appointing manager, but the job was still advertised.

The groups of staff eligible to apply depended on the type of job. In complex organisations some jobs were advertised locally, some nationally and others globally. The cost of relocation often restricted the wider advertising of lower level jobs. In some cases, the process was sequential, starting with a local ad and then moving out to other parts of the business only if necessary.

For some professional/technical jobs, qualifications formed part of the eligibility criteria.

Some organisations still kept the concept of an agreed time at which an individual will move job — rather like the 'tours of duty' common among expatriate workforces. These organisations had 'windows' of time in which staff were expected to apply for other jobs.

The Civil Service has a history of declaring whether a vacancy is open for a promotion move or only for lateral moves. This is a result of its earlier system of promotion boards. The job filling process was somewhat different in these two cases. The private sector did not make this distinction.

In some organisations, 'displaced' staff (*ie* those in need of redeployment) were given advance notification of a vacancy at their existing level (24 hours in one organisation and a week in another). In other organisations such staff and those returning from secondments or maternity leave had to apply for vacancies through the open system in the ordinary way.

Job descriptions were generated in different ways, ranging from a centrally held 'bank' of JDs which were automatically appended to the ad, to JDs generated at the time by the line manager and/or HR. A link with the job evaluation system often constrained the format and content of job descriptions, making them a poor vehicle for 'selling' the vacancy.

In addition to a job description, most job ads contained a contact point for further information and said something about the selection criteria or the skills/competencies sought. It was not always clear to employees whether they were being encouraged to ring the contact point. Some managers felt that inappropriate applications would be reduced if staff were less shy about telephoning the contact point for a better understanding of the job.

3.4.2 Application

Application forms were a central part of the process and often quite lengthy (six pages or so) and time consuming to complete. One organisation removed the applicant's name and all personal details from the form before it went to the manager for shortlisting. In another example, the application form was very restricted: to a few lines of input from both the candidate and their line manager, because there was almost total reliance on data from the appraisal process.

In the majority of cases, recent appraisals were picked up by HR and fed into the shortlisting process, as were comments from the current line manager. One organisation used several internal referees (nominated by the applicant) instead of just the current line manager.

Organisations were beginning to use on-line applications *ie* the employee submitted their application form electronically. A minority were also starting to use online CVs as part of the application to reduce the need to fill in a complex application form for each vacancy. A larger group of employers hoped to move this way in due course.

3.4.3 Selection

Shortlisting was usually done by the appointing line manager, sometimes with HR. In one case in the public sector, the appointing manager was not involved in selection at all. In some Civil Service organisations an appointment panel of two or three people was used for selection, and this would usually convene at the shortlisting stage.

Interviews were nearly always used, usually conducted by the appointing manager, sometimes with HR and/or another line manager.

Assessment centres were not normally used in filling internal vacancies. They were, however, often used as part of the process of assessing potential for senior management, and so would influence senior appointments. Tests were only occasionally used in internal selection.

The criteria used in shortlisting were not always explicit, but those used in the final selection most often were. However, candidates were not always told the selection criteria. Some scoring system was usually used in selection, although this was much more rigid in some organisations than others. Public sector organisations tend to use the most mechanical scoring systems, partly because they are more open to scrutiny. They also quite often selected purely on generic competencies and not on technical competencies.

Although most organisations claimed they gave feedback after both shortlisting and final selection, this was mostly on request and quite often informal. It could be done by the appointing manager or HR or the chair of an appointing panel.

3.4.4 Appointment

There was seldom a clear process for communicating the results of an appointment to the wider workforce.

In about half the organisations surveyed, managers could refuse to release someone who was offered another job. Grounds for this included: 'operational reasons', 'business needs' and too short a time spent in their current job. Even where managers could refuse to let someone go for a lateral move, it was made very difficult for them to refuse someone a move which would involve promotion.

Hand-over was a matter for negotiation. Where organisations set time limits of the hand-over period, the limit had rapidly become the norm as managers held onto to their staff for as long as possible while they started filling the new vacancy.

3.4.5 Monitoring and support

All the organisations had some written guidance on the OIJM process, increasingly on their intranets. Staff did not always know where this information was and were quite often confused about the finer detail of the selection process.

The central HR function often had a role in monitoring the operation of the OIJM. Some data was collected, for example tear-off slips on the bottom of application forms containing information on race and disability. Much of the data collected was never analysed. Focus groups and staff surveys were sometimes held to collect views on the process, but these were seldom compared with factual information on who was applying for and getting jobs.

Some organisations trained both managers and employees in the operation of the OIJM system. This was often done when the system was first established, but was not always repeated for new joiners or new managers or those needing a refresher.

One of the most significant differences between organisations was in the role of HR in the OIJM. In some organisations, the HR function acted as an adviser to the line throughout the process and could influence it, especially at the shortlisting stage. In others, HR set the 'rules' and left managers to operate them.

The link with HR planning was not easy to identify. An awareness of the broader resourcing context could be fed into the appointing manager by the HR manager, if their involvement was a close one. If not, line managers tended to treat each vacancy in isolation from broader resourcing issues.

3.4.6 Duration of the process

The sequence of activities described above took quite some time to complete. Internal job advertisements were posted for two to three weeks in most cases.

Once the appointment process was complete, a few organisations had a brief waiting time in case any staff wished to appeal.

A significant part of the elapsed time was the hand-over period. This was often around four weeks, but as long as six weeks in a couple of cases.

The overall time to fill a job through the OIJM process varied from three weeks to three months, with several organisations claiming their process took about two months.

3.4.7 The use of technology

With the rapid increase in electronic communication, there were differences in how far organisations had gone down the road of an electronic OIJM.

The majority of organisations involved in this project were already placing internal job ads on their intranets. This did not, however, always make them easy to find. One global business had 54 internal web sites where job ads might be found, and it was up to staff to search them. Some staff preferred seeing paper-based ads which they could browse in their own time. They also wanted computer based systems to have better searching facilities so they did not have to scroll through many screens of vacancy information to find the kind of posts they were interested in.

A few organisations had gone the extra step of encouraging on-line applications or having on-line CVs which could be pulled in as part of a job application. There is also scope to pick up more background information on both jobs and applicants from computerised databases. At present much of the collation of job applications is still an administrative task for the personnel function.

Two developments are in the pipeline. Employees would welcome the chance to leave details of the kinds of jobs they are looking for and then be contacted when jobs of this type come up. Several organisations were considering this kind of system.

There is also the possibility of using partially automated shortlisting or selection systems, as have already been developed for graduate recruitment. These will have to be very good to have any credibility with employees — a crude keyword search, for example, would not be appropriate.

3.4.8 Public and private sector differences

Within widely varying practices, there are a couple of features of OIJMs more associated with public sector or ex-public sector organisations. Procedures in the public sector tend to be more tightly defined but therefore appear more complicated. Their rigidity can also leave managers little scope for adjusting the process to meet local needs. This rigidity applies especially to what information is taken into account, and in the strict use of scored competence-based assessments.

These practices are a result of the importance of fairness and diversity in the public sector. The need to prove that a system is fair tends to lead to the mentality of following a set of 'rules'. Public sector unions have also taken this line and union negotiations have often led to some of the most complex policies.

The second striking feature of the public sector organisations involved in this study was that the HR function was often much more remote from the process than in the private sector. HR tended to set and 'police' the rules but not act so much as an adviser to the line.

These two features combine to make public sector processes often more explicit than those in the private sector. However, they can also give the whole process a very bureaucratic feel, in which the rules themselves seem to become more important than the needs of the users or the business.

This chapter of the report has painted a picture of how open internal job markets are operated. The Appendix gives a checklist which organisations can use to look at their own practices.

The next chapter highlights some of the issues and concerns faced by managers and employees when using OIJM processes.

4. Issues and Concerns in the Operation of OIJMs

Here we identify some of the issues which lay just beneath the surface of the processes described in Chapter 3. When staff or managers criticised the process, it was usually one or more of these underlying issues which were really concerning them.

4.1 Issues identified by key players

As shown by the case studies in Chapter 2, those directly involved in open job markets found the principal of open job advertising attractive, but raised a lot of practical issues. A short summary of some of the most important ones are given here.

Line managers involved in filling vacancies were concerned about:

● attracting the right the number and quality of applicants
● the time taken to fill a job and the amount of paperwork involved
● whether the process led to a good quality selection decision
● losing staff they might have wished to keep, especially if the resulting vacancy was going to be hard to fill or a long gap was likely
● too much or too little job movement.

Employees were concerned about:

● whether advertised jobs were really open or whether managers already had candidates in mind and were just 'going through the motions'

- very formalised application forms and interviews, usually competence based, which felt ritualised ('like playing a game') and did not seem to take account of their track record
- the possibility of getting stuck in a job for too long
- the squeezing out of development through 'best fit' approaches to selection
- the lack of honest feedback and career advice.

HR managers were concerned about:

- the rigour, transparency and fairness of the process
- their own workload
- groups of people or jobs for which the open system did not work well
- combining an open job market with succession planning.

The rest of this chapter examines these issues in more depth.

4.2 Keeping bureaucracy under control

Managers and employees were very concerned about the work involved for them in operating an open system. Managers spent time drafting job descriptions, dealing with queries, shortlisting and interviewing and then negotiating hand-over arrangements. Filling one vacancy could take several days of a manager's time. They also spent time dealing with the applications their own staff were making.

'Applying can be an annoying and punishing experience for employees.'

Employees found scanning for vacancies and completing application forms time consuming. Although going for one job might take only a day or two, staff who had to apply for many vacancies to secure a move found the repetition of the process time-consuming, stressful and very frustrating.

Both managers and employees talked about 'bureaucracy'. This usually referred to competence-based application forms and interviews which had become rather over-elaborate or rigid. Some processes were so complex that employees did not really understand how they worked.

The other aspect of efficiency which was of particular concern to managers was the long elapsed time between advertising a vacancy and having a replacement in post. This was especially difficult if the first round of advertising did not yield a good enough candidate. Managers who complained bitterly about this, however, were also hanging onto their own staff for as long as possible!

All in all, an open job system takes longer and generates more work than a manager simply deciding who they want to appoint. The personnel function has sometimes (but not always) saved itself some work, but this and more has been passed to line managers and employees. It may be a good way of filling jobs, but is too often both laborious and slow.

4.3 Getting the right applicants

An OIJM should in theory widen the field of candidates considered for vacancies, but it does not automatically generate the right quantity or quality of applicants. We saw cases where managers got too few applications and others where they were inundated.

'There should be a balance between a proforma and a creative advert. The advert should be creative to gain interest but also standardised with a job description.'

Considerable skill is required by the person who is filling the job, in guessing how attractive the job will be and how wide or narrow to couch the job specification. Very rigid systems which predetermine eligibility criteria and competence requirements may in some sense be 'fair', but they are not effective in attracting a candidate pool of the right quality and quantity. One organisation with a very automated system for producing job descriptions for internal ads generated far too many unsuitable applications. Job ads are almost universally dry and unappealing. No-one seems to regard them as 'selling' vehicles the way they would with an external job ad.

One organisation had a useful procedure for advertising vacancies among temporary staff if suitable permanent staff did not apply.

OIJMs seem to have exaggerated the tendency of some jobs being over-glamorised and others being seen as 'no go areas'. This is partly because the job you are in is seen to influence your chances of getting another.

The Civil Service adds another layer of complexity by differentiating between jobs which are only open for lateral movement and those which can be applied for by those in grades below. So managers have to decide before they know who is going to apply whether they can attract candidates who are already at that level. The private sector seems to live quite happily without this distinction.

4.4 Information used in selection

At the heart of the OIJM process lies the way various types of information are collated and used in shortlisting and selection. There was general acceptance on the use of a number of sources of information: the application form, recent performance reviews and the views of the current line manager.

Issues arising were:

- the skill of the applicant and the amount of practice they have had in the process becoming too dominant. Examples of this given were: nicely word processed forms doing better than hand written ones; experience at writing about competencies and responding to competence based interview questions.

'Managers like the competency approach but people have been competency interviewed to death.'

- the use of scores against competencies derived from performance appraisal in the current job role. These raised issues about whether the competencies scored in appraisal were the same set required for the vacancy (if both processes allow a subset of competencies to be considered); and whether scores are reliable enough to be used in this way.

- whether some kinds of data, for example sickness absence records, were important evidence or whether they should be excluded as potentially discriminatory.

- information on skills sometimes being restricted to generic competencies and completely ignoring job specific skills. This did not seem an appropriate approach where jobs required some very specific skills or aptitudes.

- where an employee is applying for a job which would involve a promotion, lack of clarity whether the decision process looks at skills required for a range of jobs at that level or just for the specific vacancy. It can make for trouble later on if someone cannot be redeployed easily at the same level.

- employees' dislike of processes which place too much emphasis on the views of their current boss. A minority of bosses block their subordinates from moving and this danger should be recognised. Some organisations contacted several past line managers or asked the applicant to name two or three internal referees in addition to their current boss.

● employees being unsure about the selection criteria being used at various stages of the process. In the more mechanistic processes, employees were very unclear whether the scoring from the shortlisting process carried through to become part of the scoring in the final selection and, if so, with what weight. The relative importance given to the varied sources of information is often unclear to candidates.

In cases where the consideration of information was based on fixed rules, managers felt they effectively had lost control over who to appoint. Some managers felt they ended up making a poor appointment because they were so constrained in which information to consider and how to assess it.

As organisations move more towards online CVs, new issues will arise. For example, will applicants still submit an application form or letter alongside their CV? Will individuals have a chance to tailor or update their CVs for each application? Will organisations shortlist people on the basis of their CVs without the individual even knowing this is happening?

4.5 Issues of timing

When employees were 'moved' by the organisation, the timing of job changes could be centrally controlled and chains of job moves could sometimes be synchronised. International organisations had this type of planning down to an art form. With an open job market, many of the issues raised were concerned with giving up some of this control over timing.

'Those with six months' experience can apply alongside those with ten years' experience, but this is not taken into consideration.'

Managers sometimes complained that staff moved job too often. Staff were more likely to feel that they could get stuck in jobs for a long time. It may be helpful to have a shared view of how long most employees should stay in post before looking for a move. This would help them know when to think about moving on.

However, one organisation which tried to formalise this into a more or less fixed duration in a job hit real problems. The idea of a 'window' of time in which the employee should look for other jobs did not always coincide with suitable vacancies being advertised. The organisation also had a rule that when an employee applied for a post they should put their own post on the market. Not surprisingly this process acted as a disincentive to apply for jobs and the whole labour market started to freeze.

Figure 4.1: The 'gap' between post holders

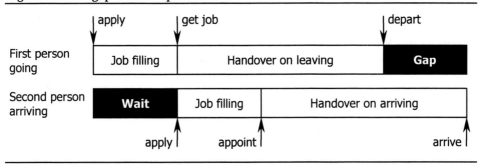

Source: IES, 2000

Trying to impose rigid timing back into an open market seems unworkable.

An open job system seems to lead inevitably to gaps between a job being vacated and the next job holder filling the gap. As Figure 4.1 shows, the length of the gap is unaffected by the length of hand-over (as long as this is always the same) and is equal to the time it takes to make the appointment. So gaps are minimised by a rapid appointment process which gets off the mark quickly once the job holder has accepted a new job.

Some groups of staff do need to find jobs at particular points in time because they will otherwise be jobless. These groups, such as returners, secondees and those in need of redeployment are discussed further in sections 4.7.

4.6 Fairness and diversity

In theory, an open system ought to be seen as fair, and indeed employees did see this as a strong argument in favour of OIJMs. However, in talking about practice, employees often raised queries about the 'fairness' of their system. Their issues included:

● whether the shortlisting and selection decision was made objectively, *ie* not taking into account whether the manager already knew someone, or had a particular candidate in mind, or preferred people from their part of the business.

● whether the selection criteria favoured some groups of staff more than others (*eg* specialists or generalists; those working in some parts of the organisation). Staff working in unglamorous jobs often felt they were overlooked in selection and also that their bosses were reluctant to let them go as it would be hard to attract a replacement. So they were doubly 'stuck'.

- staff with long service in their current post also felt it was hard to get a move, and they could block opportunities for others. The length of service of candidates in their current posts is not normally considered as a selection criteria. However, managers have concerns about people who are persistent 'runners up' for vacancies. Open job markets do not deal well with people who are simply 'overdue' for a job move.

- whether the process itself was harder for some people than others. For example, one company had found that older people took longer to adjust to giving evidence in terms of competencies. Staff who are made unduly nervous by interviews may also be at a disadvantage.

- staff felt a system was fair if they felt they 'had a good shot' at getting the job. Central to this was an application and interview process which gave them space to make their case, and then feedback on why they had not got the job if they failed.

- whether the process guarded against discrimination on grounds of personal characteristics: age, gender, disability, race *etc.* Indirect discrimination was also cause for concern, for example if staff from ethnic minorities have been concentrated in certain jobs where competencies were more difficult to develop. Part-timers were another group of concern.

- in an open system, you have to be in the right place at the right time when a vacancy comes up and you have to spot it. You also have to gauge whether it is worth applying, not knowing who else will go for it or what the manager is really looking for. There is an element of luck in all this which was sometimes felt to be unfair.

'The company would be poorer without the open system and it would lead to equal opportunities problems. Equal opportunities is the system's greatest contribution.'

We found little hard evidence that the OIJM is any more or less 'fair' than a more managed movement system. A feedback system which requires managers to explain decisions to individuals is an important safeguard. Overall monitoring of outcomes is very important, but not often conducted on a regular basis. Several companies felt that an open system made the failure to get a job more visible and employees therefore tended to perceive many instances in which a good candidate failed to get a job. The DTI case study showed that a system could be much 'fairer' than staff perceived it to be.

4.7 Disadvantaged groups

A number of groups of staff are at some disadvantage in an open job market.

- Staff displaced by organisational change often have limited time in which to seek redeployment, depending on the redundancy policy of the organisation. Sometimes their redeployment is managed, sometimes they are given the first shot at vacancies, and sometimes they just have to use the same system as everyone else. In a highly devolved system, managers may be reluctant to take them if there are better candidates around. Staff felt that being on a redeployment list carried some stigma.

- Other groups with limited time to find a job are returners from maternity leave, career breaks or secondments. They have the additional disadvantage of being outside the organisation while looking for a job inside it. Getting hold of vacancy information, networking and attending interviews can all be problematic. The organisation may have changed if they have been outside it for a few years, and even the language of the job ads may be difficult to understand. They may also have no understanding of the OIJM process itself. As a minimum, these groups need some fallback by which they can secure a satisfactory job in the short term and then maybe look around for something better. Those returning from developmental secondments and courses (*eg* MBAs) were quite shocked that, in being left to find their own jobs, their organisations seemed indifferent as to whether their new skills were put to good use.

- Other groups are disadvantaged because they may appear less attractive to managers or only have a narrow range of job options. Part-timers often felt it was not worth applying for jobs when the manager really wanted a full-timer. Those who were overdue for a move also felt managers did not look at them positively.

- Finally, there were concerns about staff who just got 'stuck' because they were not very good at performing in the selection system or were always 'runner up.' In theory such people could wait indefinitely for a job move under a fully open system.

Organisations have quite difficult choices to make about whether to intervene with managed moves for such groups, or whether the HR function can improve their chances of success by a combination of additional advice and informal influence on line managers.

4.8 Managed moves in an open job market

As we have seen above there are a number of groups of staff who may, on occasion, need a managed job move, *ie* one which is not filled via the open process.

Other reasons for managed moves may include:

- local redeployment within a team of staff at the same grade level. This helps with work allocation and also with development. Arrangements are often in place to allow for such movement being locally agreed between the manager and his or her team.
- the planned job experience of trainees (*eg* graduate or professional trainees). Specific posts are quite often held outside the normal system for developing trainees who will move through them in rotation. Usually only small numbers of people are involved in such moves.
- appointments very near the top of the business, which are often outside the open system (although the level of open appointments has risen over time). Such appointments may be planned some time ahead through formal or informal succession planning.
- developmental job moves for mid-career staff identified as high potential, which are more contentious than the other categories above. Such moves may be the result of succession planning which has identified particular job experiences required by an individual.

'Managed moves and open internal recruitment both have a place but companies need to work out how they fit together.'

It is this last category, rather than the few jobs at the very top, which gave rise to much debate in the workshops about the best way of running succession planning in parallel with an open market. The moves concerned are, by definition, often into business areas or functions of which the candidate has little prior experience. The jobs are often high profile, do not exist in large numbers and would be highly prized by other candidates already working in that area.

Two different approaches are used. In the first, developmental moves are made which override the normal open process. In the second, candidates identified through succession plans are invited to apply alongside other candidates and a judgement is made as to whether to appoint them once the other candidates have come forward and interviews have been held.

In a variant of this second approach, candidates identified through succession plans are treated as 'preferred' and other applicants are told there is a preferred candidate at the time the post is advertised.

The presence of a high potential candidate does, however, inevitably change the nature of the decision, as a balance is being made between longer-term potential and short-term performance.

This issue of the weight given to development in an internal job market is one of the strategic balances discussed in the concluding chapter of this report.

4.9 How open is open?

This study has shown that the openness of internal job markets is usually constrained in two ways:

- Jobs are more often advertised across part of the organisation than all of it. Only the most senior roles or those which are very hard to fill are advertised globally. Managers are often given considerable flexibility to re-deploy their resources locally and at the same grade level without having to advertise posts.

- Managed moves, as discussed above, are used to some degree to resolve specific problems or to engineer the career development of key people.

These limitations make sense both to managers and employees. However, the research also showed that employees were sensitive to the proportion of jobs taken out of the open system. It is hard to put a figure on what is acceptable. One organisation which had about 70 per cent of its jobs advertised (excluding very local re-deployment) was seen to be reasonable by its staff. Another, where the proportion was more like 50 per cent, was definitely seen by its employees as 'only advertising the unattractive jobs'.

Where managers already had a candidate in mind for a vacancy, several organisations still advertised the job and personnel managers claimed that the preferred candidate was not always appointed. The signalling of a preferred candidate in the job application was appreciated by employees, who preferred to know the real situation.

'Advertising
posts that are
not really open
just raises
expectations
and wastes
people's time.'

In one case, there were always long lists of job vacancies but only very short lists announcing posts which had been filled. This made staff very suspicious that many of the advertised posts were in fact being filled another way, and undermined their confidence in the system.

While open jobs markets do not have to operate for all jobs, employees will become very cynical if too many exceptions are made. Tolerance of jobs being filled outside the open system is obviously lower in organisations where opportunities for promotion are limited.

4.10 The role of HR

The role played by HR in an OIJM process varied considerably in the organisations involved in this research. A key issue for HR people was how to position their role to add most value to the process without over-managing or over-policing the line managers who predominantly take selection decisions.

HR can be involved in a variety of ways:

- policy setting and the production of material which communicates policy
- training employees, managers and panel members
- supporting managers in drafting job ads, setting selection criteria, and designing interview questions
- support to individual employees having difficulty with the system or wanting career advice
- making appropriate connections with groups requiring special attention (*eg* those needing redeployment, returners, secondees) and with career management processes (*eg* succession and high potential development)
- direct involvement in shortlisting and selection
- administration of ads, applications, collation of additional information (*eg* performance reviews), panels (if used) and appointments
- quality control of specific activities, getting feedback from users and monitoring outcomes.

The administrative workload for HR is still considerable in most organisations and there is still a challenge in using IT to make the process run smoothly, quickly and with less paper shuffling. Introducing open job markets had not of itself reduced workload or headcount in HR, and had sometimes increased it.

There were differences between organisations in how centralised the OIJM process was and how much it could be adjusted to meet local or job specific needs. Managers appreciated the flexibility to adjust the process, for example in one case they were free to use appropriate selection tests if they wished to. However, staff still need a broadly similar process across the organisation if they are to get the benefits of being able to apply for jobs in different work areas.

A deeper issue is whether HR best ensures the quality of the process by working directly with managers at various stages of the process, or by setting and 'policing' a set of rules. A compromise, quite common in the private sector, was that HR would be only cursorily involved in the majority of vacancies (*eg* in scanning job descriptions) but could be called in by managers where they needed more support. HR might also be able to influence moves for high potential people or those with difficulties in securing a suitable move.

Optimists might hope the role of HR would diminish over time as employees and managers become more confident in an open approach. At present, employees still feel that the role of HR is crucial in ensuring 'fair play.'

4.11 Evaluating an OIJM system

Evaluation was not mentioned very often by those interviewed in the course of this project. However, given some of the issues raised above it would seem important to know what is working and not working in an OIJM; whether it is fair or unfairly operated; whether minority groups are improving their representation at senior levels; and how much it is all costing. So the IES research team identified an issue of monitoring almost because of its absence.

Several organisations collected information which could be used for monitoring, but it was not always analysed. Where the process was evaluated, staff focus groups were sometimes held, but canvassing the views of significant numbers of staff was rare. Organisations using staff attitude surveys do not usually include sufficiently specific or probing questions on the job filling process to find out what is working and what is not.

The DTI case study in Chapter 2 describes a more comprehensive approach to evaluation, including a staff survey as well as focus groups and considerable analysis of factual data on job moves and job applicants. One would not seek to carry out such a comprehensive review more than every few years, but hard data could be monitored at least annually. Random checks on key processes (*eg* job ads, shortlisting, interviews, feedback) would also be useful.

Evaluation is important if processes are to be improved, but also increases staff confidence in the system.

In the concluding chapter we will return to the original research questions and examine what we might mean by 'good practice' in the operation of open internal job markets.

5. Conclusions: A Matter of Balance

5.1 Do open job markets work?

This project started with a series of questions:

- Are open internal job markets an effective and efficient means of deploying skills in the organisation?
- Do they help or hinder the skill development of the workforce?
- What are their side effects (*eg* on the amount of job movement, career paths, diversity, morale, retention *etc*.)?
- How is the process explained to users?
- What roles are played by the HR function in the operation of an open internal job market?

The detailed case studies and wider debate show that the answers to these questions are not clear cut.

OIJMs can be a more effective way of deploying skills if advertising goes wide enough and if staff feel they can apply for jobs outside their immediate work area. Factors which inhibit effective deployment include managers who block or discourage staff from applying for vacancies, and appointing managers who are only interested in candidates they already know. The way a job is described and the selection criteria used also have a key effect on whether the process deploys skills effectively. We saw some cases in which skills important to the job were not considered and poor selection decisions were made.

The efficiency of an OIJM is probably more in doubt than its effectiveness. Although HR people proclaim proudly that central personnel administration has been reduced, a large cost is incurred through the time spent by candidates applying for jobs and managers shortlisting and then interviewing. In some organisations HR workload had increased. None of the organisations involved in the research has really costed the process. Several felt that employees often applied for vacancies for which they were unsuitable. An efficient OIJM relies on well-equipped users. Some organisations had processes which took a long time (three months to fill a job) and suffered big gaps between post-holders.

Workforce development is certainly not delivered by many of the processes we have seen operated. There is always a temptation for managers to appoint the candidate who can 'hit the ground running'. Formal processes of selection magnify this trend in the operation of OIJMs if they operate mechanical scoring systems which rate candidates against specific skills. Such a system can seem the most fair, but can easily squeeze out development. Developmental moves then occur as exceptions to the system and can lead to a two tier system: managed moves for the best and the OIJM for the rest.

The wider impact of an OIJM again depends on how it is implemented. Most staff like the idea of this approach, so it should have a positive effect on morale. This turned sour if managers were thought to be acting unfairly or if the procedure was so bureaucratic as to put staff off the whole process. In some cases the rate of job movement was felt to be too high and in others too low. This was partly a consequence of wider factors (eg rates of turnover and growth, or contraction in staffing levels), but also depended on whether staff were helped to use the system wisely, and whether they were put off by the bureaucracy of the process. In a similar way, some organisations had a healthy number of lateral moves and cross-boundary moves occurring. In others, this flexibility was reduced by managers behaving parochially or the system placing undue limitations on which jobs staff could apply for. In the one case where hard data was available, an open job market was found to favour diversity, although staff perceptions were that women and ethnic minorities were treated less favourably.

Procedures are generally set down in documents (paper or electronic), but many of the staff interviewed still felt there were aspects of the process they did not fully understand. Formal training in operating the system was not always adequate or timely.

As the process tends to be quite complex, it is very helpful if the HR function offers support to the line and is also available to offer advice to individuals. The quality of an OIJM process lies not in the rules set, but in how the HR function provides support. This research showed glimpses of a nightmare scenario in which rules become more and more complex and more strictly applied while the users become increasingly confused and disempowered and poor selection decisions are made.

This research has not identified a single model of 'best practice', but rather a number of elements of sensible practice which need to fit together. The rest of this chapter examines these elements.

5.2 The importance of context

The case studies showed that some OIJM systems are better accepted than others. However, the level of acceptance and satisfaction was heavily influenced by a number of contextual factors outside the OIJM system itself. These included:

- the previous system for filling internal vacancies, and whether it was seen as having operated effectively and fairly. Although some employees were reluctant to accept responsibility for their own careers, they did not always see the past through rose tinted glasses.

- where the shift to an OIJM coincided with a radical decentralisation of personnel management. This could leave employees feeling somewhat vulnerable, and some managers feeling unsupported.

- OIJM processes require an open culture and one in which there are high levels of trust between employees and line managers. Previously secretive and bureaucratic cultures take some time to adjust to a more open style of management.

- as a related factor, the level of people management skill among line managers. OIJMs depend on managers having both the competence and the inclination to carry out a difficult process with care and good judgement.

- situations where grade, and therefore promotion, were seen as crucial. These organisations suffered from people applying for jobs at higher grades for which they were not suitable.

- recognition that an OIJM cannot, in the short term, correct an over-supply or under-supply of good quality applicants. Organisations which were short of skills found internal poaching a problem. Conversely, where staff were over-skilled for their current grade and promotion opportunities were scarce, an OIJM simply confronted employees with their frustration. When major change is taking place and lots of staff are seeking redeployment, the open system may have to be put on hold.

- in most organisations, jobs in unpopular locations or which are perceived as onerous or boring. Again an OIJM highlights these problems, but has not caused them. Indeed one can argue that an open system gives managers a stronger incentive to make their jobs attractive to the best candidates.

- the relative need for and valuing of specialist and generalist skills. In some cases a selection system based on generic skills was at odds with the organisation's need for more specialists. In other cases, specialists had access to generalist jobs, but movement in the opposite direction was of necessity difficult. This was not a problem caused by the OIJM, but by the need for different skill sets within the organisation.

5.3 Monitoring, communication and support

Although 'best practice' may be hard to define, the general processes of monitoring, communication and support were fundamental to how well the OIJM functioned in those organisations involved in this research.

Most of the criticisms of OIJM processes by staff amounted to the process being too complex or confusing, or line managers not being open. So communication is key to good practice. It is linked with monitoring and practical support. Some elements of good practice in these areas are:

- clear descriptions of the general process and general training for staff in its operation

- clear and accurate information about each particular vacancy. Information about whether there are preferred candidates for a particular post.

- feedback to all applicants for jobs and access to further advice and coaching if they need it

- open communication on how specific vacancies have been filled

- opportunities for staff and managers to give feedback on the process

- publishing of monitoring information on how the system is performing
- training and advice to those involved in drafting ads, shortlisting and selection.

5.4 A matter of balance

Beyond these general process aspects of good practice, which of the many alternative combinations of practice will work best? The study suggests that good practice may lie in striking an appropriate balance on the inevitable tensions at work in an OIJM. Some of the key tensions are shown in .

Each of the six features shown as the outer ring on this diagram is desirable. However, taken to extreme, any feature can compromise the others. Although there are trade-offs between all the features shown, some of the strongest tensions lie between pairs of factors as follows:

- Processes which are very **rigorous** and can be proved to operate to a set of rules become very unwieldy and do not have the flexibility to deal with changing needs.Figure 5.1
- Processes which **deploy skills** so as to always appoint the 'best person for the job' will squeeze out workforce development.
- Processes which are strongly **line owned** can lack sufficient controls, but conversely, a process which is over-controlled by HR deprives the line of real responsibility for their decisions.

Figure 5.1: A matter of balance

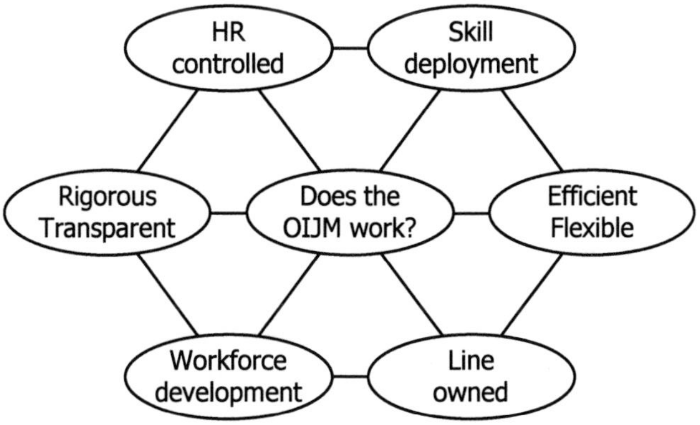

Source: IES, 2000

5.5 Balancing rigour with efficiency

An over-rigorous process, such as those seen in some parts of the Civil Service, becomes so rule-bound that employees comment that they are 'playing a game' or 'jumping through hoops'. The rules are followed even when managers know they are leading to a poor selection decision. The mechanistic use of competencies was a central problem with over-tight processes, as was the over-reliance on a single source of evidence (especially if it was performance review scores).

> 'The open system is fair but does not remove the possibility of managers picking the ones they like and getting them to apply. This is not about changing the system but about educating the managers.'

Users need to remain aware that they are dealing with subjective information and be trained to handle such information with confidence and good judgement. They also need to be wary of selecting people who are skilled at using the system but who may not be the best candidates. Rule-bound processes also become very time consuming for both applicants and managers and involve huge quantities of paperwork, repeated for each vacancy.

Employees are equally worried by insufficiently rigorous processes. They commented in such cases that managers still appoint their preferred candidates and just 'go through the motions' of advertising.

Balance in this dimension is about blending rules with judgement and taking a holistic view of both the people and the job. It is also about not tolerating managers who abuse the system by, for

Figure 5.2: Balancing rigour with efficiency

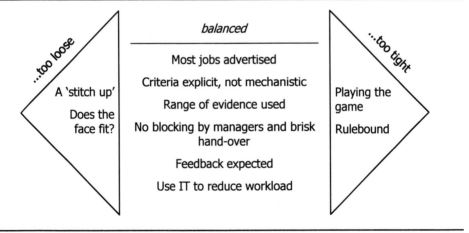

Source: IES, 2000

The Institute for Employment Studies

example, blocking their staff or delaying hand-over. Feedback and monitoring processes are a useful way of ensuring decisions can be justified. The tendency to form-filling and excessive paperwork can also be reduced by the increasing use of IT for communication and data retrieval.

5.6 Balancing deployment with development

Most OIJM processes are set up to select the person with the skills closest to those needed by the job. Almost by default, this process gives rise to the Catch 22 of the OIJM: 'if you haven't done the job before you will not be allowed to try doing it'. This is fundamentally at odds with the need to continuously develop the workforce and respond to changing business needs by exercising flexibility in the internal labour market.

In at least one case, the need to maximise a score on a specified competence profile for the job was badly distorting the performance review process which generated these scores. Other organisations suffered from job specs which were so bland that far too many applications were received from people who were unsuitable for the job.

The happy medium lies in the careful setting of selection criteria to allow space for development. Criteria should normally cover both job specific (technical) and general skill requirements. It

Figure 5.3: Balancing deployment with development

...too loose

Anyone can apply for anything

balanced

Realistic job specs

Technical and generic skills

Some planned and explained developmental moves

Open project opportunities and secondments

Building development into 'normal' appointments

...too tight

Hitting the ground running

Distorted HRM

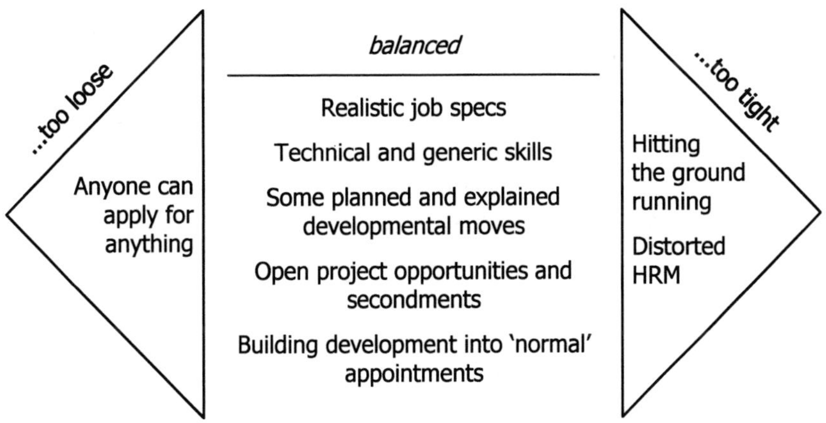

Source: IES, 2000

would also help to clarify which skills are essential for the job and which desirable.

It would help if jobs ads could be more explicit about the opportunity for development within the job, just as is often done when advertising externally.

'No-one wants to make developmental appointments — they are too busy and stressed.'

Managers do need support for building development back in. At present they are given every incentive to pick staff who can do the job immediately, even if this is detrimental to the longer-term health of the organisation.

All the organisations involved in the workshops felt they needed some managed moves for some types of development. The complex issue of running managed moves alongside an open job market has been discussed in Chapter 4. The learning point is that managed moves can only be used in small numbers without throwing an open job market into disrepute. Managed moves cannot substitute for a developmental component built into 'normal' (*ie* open) job moves.

Additional development is increasingly available at work through project working and sometimes also secondments (internal or external). Some organisations were becoming more open about such opportunities and encouraging staff to apply for them in roughly the same way as for job vacancies.

5.7 Balancing line ownership with HR control

The final of the three balances suggested by our research is perhaps the most important of all, as it supports the other two. The challenge for the HR function is to ensure the quality of the OIJM process without over-policing the system.

The actions required to achieve this balance relate back to what we said earlier in this chapter about monitoring, communication and support. Quality can be achieved in three main ways:

● through rules
● through persuasion in the form of information, training and advice
● through monitoring and open communication of outcomes.

The research showed some grim examples of an unworkable rule being ever more strongly enforced, *eg* in expecting employees to pre-plan the precise timing of their moves in an open job system.

'We feel we have the right balance of rules, advice, support, involvement, and facilitation. Line managers will come to HR for advice.'

A strong HR advisory function was much valued by managers and employees alike. It gave them much more confidence in the system and allowed for a more responsive process. This was why OIJM systems did not always lead to dramatic reductions in personnel workload. Independent panel members can provide some impartial input to sift and selection, but are less likely to bring the same range of expertise as HR people who are continuously involved in resourcing issues. Most of the private sector employers saw a strong HR advisory function as vital, although this message was sometimes unpalatable to the public sector organisations hoping for less hands-on involvement of HR.

In particular, managers are right to look to the HR function for extra help with jobs which are hard to fill, or people who are repeatedly applying for the wrong jobs or failing to obtain job moves. The flexibility to deal with the minority of jobs and people which cause difficulties obviates the need for extra rules unnecessary for the majority.

In the scheme of things, very few of the organisations involved in this project put much effort into monitoring the outcomes of OIJM processes. Line managers who know data is collected on who has applied for jobs and who has been appointed are likely

Figure 5.4: Balancing line ownership with HR control

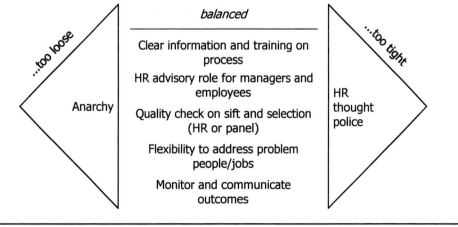

Source: IES, 2000

Free, Fair and Efficient?

to take care over the process. Although one does not like to talk in terms of 'naming and shaming', consistent, low-key monitoring can be cheaper and more appropriate than other more intrusive 'policing' methods.

5.8 Think about outcomes, not procedures

The final aspect of good practice we want to highlight is about the mindset with which HR professionals and line managers approach the operation of an OIJM. Many people we interviewed saw the problem as one of setting correct procedures and then following them. In other words, they saw the operation of an OIJM as essentially as administrative matter.

Most organisations would do better to think about internal job filling as a decision-making process, not just a set of rules and procedures which a manager must follow. The kinds of questions which are important are: What do we really want from the person who will take this job? Do we need someone who can 'hit the ground running' or is it an opportunity to develop someone? How can the job ad encourage the right kinds of applicants? What selection criteria will we prioritise? What would each candidate bring to the team as well as to their own job?

There is also a striking difference between the resources, creativity and judgement applied to external recruitment and that applied to internal vacancy filling.

Procedures for operating an OIJM should be designed to help managers think about their decision, not as a kind of auto-pilot which makes managers suspend their normal judgement.

A mindset based more on outcomes and less on procedures might encourage more lively and interesting advertisements. It might also help to put some of the fundamentalist use of competencies in perspective. Just as recruiters are always looking to use the external labour market better, so effective organisations need to become experts at making best use of their internal labour markets. As organisational change continues, the ability to both deploy and develop staff internally is vital to success. The internal job market is where these crucial decisions are made.

5.9 Pointers to good practice

This report has shown that practices vary considerably in the operation of open internal job markets, and it is difficult to be definitive about what works best. However, we would suggest the following pointers on the basis of this exploratory research:

- Take account of the business and personnel management context in designing the process. Of particular importance is the willingness and skill of line managers to take responsibility for filling job vacancies.

- Produce clear descriptions of the general process and general training for staff in its operation, plus in-depth training and advice to those involved in drafting ads, shortlisting and selection.

- If several similar vacancies occur at one time, run one process advertising them together.

- If using electronic ads, ensure they can be easily found and searched. Use technology to reduce the need to repeat information (*eg* by online applications and posting CVs).

- Produce clear and accurate information about each particular vacancy, and general background information on types of job.

- Selection criteria should cover both generic and technical skills and be known to the candidates. They should clarify which skills are essential and which desirable. Competence-based applications and interviews should be user-friendly and not too rigid.

- Involve someone who is independent in shortlisting and interviews alongside the line manager, *eg* an HR manager or panel member from another work area.

- Use multiple sources of evidence in decisions. Data on track record is extremely important and should not rely exclusively on numerical competence scores from appraisal or the views of the current line manager.

- When promoting an individual, consider their suitability for the grade not just the single post they are applying for.

- Build an element of development into open ads and appointments, as you would with external recruitment.

- If some developmental moves are made outside the open system, communicate about this clearly. Ensure the clear majority of jobs are still openly advertised.

- Provide additional support to those who need redeployment, returners, secondees and those who are 'stuck'.

- Indicate openly whether there is a preferred candidate for a particular post at the point it is advertised.

- Provide feedback to all applicants for jobs, and access to further advice and coaching if they need it.

- Do not tolerate line managers who abuse the system or block their own staff from moving jobs.

- Communicate openly on how specific vacancies have been filled.

- Create opportunities for staff and managers to give feedback from time to time on the process, *eg* through staff surveys.

- Regularly publish monitoring information on how the system is performing in terms of outcomes.

- Think of the whole process as a decision, not a set of rules.

Appendix: Checklist for Reviewing an OIJM Process

Advertisement

Is there a clear process for deciding how to handle each vacancy as it arises? Is there a quick and simple process for obtaining approval to fill a vacancy?

Are similar job vacancies occurring close in time grouped together into a single round of advertising?

How does the process of advertising externally link with the OIJM (*eg* in parallel or sequence; what triggers, decision to look outside)?

What proportion of vacancies are advertised? Which ones are 'managed'? Are there clear criteria for such decisions? Are staff informed if a job is filled without internal advertisement?

Are project opportunities, secondments *etc.* advertised along with permanent posts?

What governs whether a job is advertised locally, nationally, or internationally, and within or across business units?

How is the job description generated? Does the job ad give: a good description of the job; indication of salary; competencies or selection criteria; contact point for more information?

If skills or competencies are listed, do they cover both generic and technical skills? Is it clear which skills are essential and which desirable?

Who judges whether the job information will encourage an appropriate volume and range of applicants?

What eligibility criteria are set when a job is advertised (*eg* length of service in current post, current grade, qualifications)?

How easy it is for staff to see advertised jobs? If electronic, can they search for jobs of a specific type? How do returners (*eg* secondees) see job ads? How long is a job posted for?

Are displaced staff or returners given advance notice of vacancies? Are good quality temporary staff given the opportunity to apply for permanent posts before going to the external market?

Can staff ask to be informed of job vacancies of specified types as they arise?

Application

Does the applicant's line manager need to approve their application? Are they asked to comment on the application?

Are developmental applicants (*eg* from a succession process) encouraged to apply?

How easy is the application form to complete? Can applications be submitted electronically?

Can staff maintain a CV which can be pulled into their job applications? Are there other ways to save staff repeating effort if they are making a number of job applications?

If evidence of competence is required on the application, is the format and language user-friendly?

What other information is collated prior to shortlisting (*eg* basic personnel record; previous performance reviews; PDPs; succession information; internal references)?

Is monitoring information collected on applicants (*eg* gender; race; age; length of service in organisation and job; current job)?

Selection

Are the steps in the selection process clear (*eg* shortlisting, interview or paper sift)?

What information is used as the basis for shortlisting (*eg* application form; internal CV; performance reviews; line manager comments or informal views; PDP)?

Who shortlists (appointing manager; other managers; HR; panel)? What encourages appointing manager to consider applicants they don't know?

How explicit are the shortlisting criteria? Is a scoring system used? How is weight given to developmental candidates or displaced/returning staff?

How do those not shortlisted get feedback? Who gives this feedback? Can it follow through to career advice or better training if candidates are making inappropriate applications?

After shortlisting, is additional data generated prior to final selection (*eg* tests, assessment centres, more information from boss or internal references)?

On what basis is the selection decision made? Is this process made explicit to candidates? If shortlisting was scored, is this carried through to final selection, and with what weight?

Is the process different for certain key promotion thresholds (*eg* how does it link with the use of assessment centres at the gateway to senior management)?

If interviews are held, who is involved (*eg* appointing manager; other managers; HR; panel)? Are questions designed in advance? Do they cover the critical aspects of the job? If competencies are discussed, do they cover the most important aspects of the job (both generic and technical)?

If panel members are used, how are they chosen so as to be impartial in the process?

Who takes the final decision? Is it based on some scoring of candidates and, if so, is it helpful or too mechanistic?

How do unsuccessful candidates get feedback? Can it follow through to career advice or better training if candidates are not interviewing well?

Is there an appeal process for candidates who feel they have been unfairly treated in an appointment process?

Appointment

Who implements the appointment decision?

How do staff not immediately involved as applicants know an appointment has been made and how it was made?

Is there an agreed maximum period between the appointment decision and the individual taking up their new post? Is it an appropriate length?

Can a manager block an individual taking up an appointment or delay it unduly?

Is there some flexibility to deal with hand-over issues?

Monitoring and support

Is clear written guidance available on the job filling process, which managers and staff can find easily at any time? If on an intranet is it clearly signposted?

Does the organisation help staff understand roughly how often they might expect to move jobs and what kinds of career paths exist?

Is there background information easily available on types of job, their content and skill requirements?

Is it clear where in the job filling process HR has a quality control and/or advisory role?

Where can individuals go if they need advice on which jobs to apply for, or how to improve their application or interviewing skills? Are repeatedly unsuccessful applicants directed to such support?

If the performance management system feeds into internal job filling, is the link clear? Is the information used reliable?

Where succession planning or special development schemes exist, how do these link with the OIJM? If individuals are discussed by a career review process of some kind, do they get useful feedback?

Is there adequate training in the OIJM process and in specific aspects of it (*eg* competence based applications and interviews) for managers, employees, HR managers and panel members?

Is there a process for sample checks on the quality of the process (*eg* content of advert; shortlisting, interviews, decision)?

Is data kept and analysed on who applies for and who gets jobs (by such factors as gender, age, length of service, race, disability, grade level)? Are the types of moves monitored, *eg* moves between departments or units — lateral as opposed to promotion moves? Is there any evidence that groups of staff are discriminated against by the process?

Do staff surveys include questions about the job filling process, especially whether it is well understood and perceived to be fair?

Is monitoring information, both factual and perception data, published to staff at regular intervals?

Is there feedback to senior managers if their part of the business is not seen as operating a fair and high quality process for the filling of jobs?

Are monitoring data and overall HRP information used to modify the process and fine-tune job ads and selection criteria?